John Mulry, Msc

DIRECT RESPONSE

7 Steps to marketing your business and prospering in this new economy...

John Mulry, MSc

Foreword by Jim Toner

John Mulry, Msc

Direct Response

What others are saying about John Mulry...

"John was lucky enough to be personally mentored and trained by me. As a GKIC Certified Business Advisor, he's equipped with an arsenal of tools that any small business owner can pick up and run with to start producing big time, bottom line results. This is exactly the kind of advice I needed when I started my career... but nobody who really knew what was going on was willing to share. If you're a business owner and you want real improvement in your business then I highly suggest you listen to what John has to say."
– Dan Kennedy, Dan Kennedy, Serial Entrepreneur, Multi Millionaire and Highest Paid Direct Response Marketer in the World

"The thing about John that most people aren't willing to do, is to actually apply the best practices that they learn to their own business and life in order to achieve maximum effectiveness in minimum time."
- Nick Nanton, CEO of the Dicks Nanton Celebrity Branding® Agency, Emmy Award Winning Director, Producer & Best-Selling Author

"If someone had told me you will get an extra €10k in your bank account from doing this [working with John], I would have laughed but yes this has transformed my business and the results were outstanding. I closed a total of 24 clients once I activated what I had learned. It totally changed by way of thinking and how to approach my marketing strategy. The results were immediate. This has made a huge impact on my business going forward. I now have a system in place I have laser-targeted marketing and am no longer just "winging it". In 8 hours the amount of marketing information I didn't know that I didn't know was just ridiculous. A lot of my business comes through Facebook and primarily referrals. However on this workshop I discovered exactly who my niche market are and that

probably 50% of them aren't on facebook and probably don't know my current clients. Well what about my website? I asked. Well you can track that, John said. And then went on to explain how to drive that missing 50% from offline to online, reel them in to get their contact information and then to entice them over 28 days to get in contact with me. This is only one example of mattered to me and this only covered 2 modules out of the ten covered that day. I don't care who you are, unless you've studied marketing or already work with someone who does your marketing for you then it's probably safe to say your just winging it. Get on board and get the information."

- **John T Kenny, Access Fitness, Dublin**

"Right from the very first interaction I had with John, which was getting his book "Truth About Marketing" all the way to someone to one consultation time, I have been blown away by the actionable advice I have received. Even if I implement just a few things he suggested, it will add €1,000's to my income over the coming months and years. He's one of the most knowledgeable and sincere marketers around."

- **Gareth Sherry**

It didn't take long for John's marketing gems to click on a few light bulbs for me and set me straight, as I put together my new advertising campaigns. Yep, light bulbs is a good metaphor - I feel as if a whole series of darkened mind corridors have been illuminated and revealed! But that's not all. John was so generous in contacting me personally to sort out some tech issues, a great reflection of his generosity in sharing his expertise and giving value to so many."

- **Audrey Wynne**

"Working with John, he helped me develop some simple but very effective sales and marketing strategies that have helped me close sales and increase revenue for my business. John's in depth knowledge of marketing and his easy to apply systems are a huge benefit to any business needing a boost. Highly recommended."

- **Don Neachtain**

"Surpassed my expectations so much that I am in awe (I have never used that word in m life). One of the most helpful contacts I have ever had with any marketing consultant and I have years of personal experience with consultants - a few in the excellent category, so I am not just comparing him to the usual ones but to the best."

- **Lee Parratt**

*"John provides quality information for anyone who is in business, or looking to get into business, concerning their marketing efforts. I follow everything John Mulry and Dan Kennedy teach in their marketing training. It is amazing what little changes they teach can do for a business." – **Brian Whitesides***

For more visit www.JohnMulry.com

John Mulry, Msc

Direct Response

ISBN-13: 978-0-9928003-2-1

Direct Response is available at special quantity discounts for bulk purchases, for sales promotions, premiums, fundraising, and educational use. For more information, please write to the below address.

Published by: Expect Success Academy
Unit 14, Ballybane Enterprise Centre
Galway, Ireland

www.JohnMulry.com

First Edition, 2016

Edited by: Jessica Thompson
www.Jessica.ie

Foreword by: Jim Toner

Cover Art by: Sam and Bax

Published in Ireland

John Mulry, Msc

To Jess, mam, my sister, family and friends...

Thanks for supporting me, I love you all and I'm eternally grateful for everything...

To you, the business owner...

Thank you for taking risks, for doing what you do and for giving it your all. EXPECT SUCCESS...

In life, you don't necessarily get what you want and you don't necessarily get what you need. Instead, you get what you honestly and truly believe you deserve. In other words, you get what you expect, so why not EXPECT SUCCESS?

–John Mulry

Table of Contents

John Mulry, Msc

Foreword by Jim Toner

I once was lost, but now I am found" -
Amazing Grace

I think that one simple, but incredibly beautiful line says it all for business owners and entrepreneurs that have "seen the light"

For most however, it is this line.

"I'm on the highway to Hell"
AC/DC

Yet another classic and totally awesome line and song...BUT...we are not talking music here, we are talking business and there is no business if there are no customers. No customers = no money.

Now I am sure everyone gets that. No customers = no money is pretty basic even for a newbie. The question is what are we DOING in order to GET the customers that put food on the table?

If you are like most business owners / entrepreneurs you most likely do one of the following 3 things.

1. Hope someone contacts you
2. Use traditional, one size fits all marketing sold to by a sales rep making $20,000 a year…and hope it works. Hint…it doesn't
3. Nothing

This my friends is why the vast majority of people with their own business fail. And I mean, most. I myself was one of those business owners albeit far more sophisticated than most.

With my field of real estate investment training and seminars I chose the mass market-advertising route and went with radio, radio shows and television. Even though it was very expensive, $20,000 - $30,000 a month, it worked…until it didn't.

A big mistake business owners make with their marketing is that they are a "one trick pony" meaning they use a medium and if it works they run with it. Now that in and of its self is not the problem, the problem is they more often than not have no backup plan. As Dan Kennedy says…"they all go lame"

That was my problem. When my advertising went "lame" it hurt in a VERY big way. It was only AFTER I had lost close to $100,000 that I realized I needed someone that was far superior to me in marketing.

I had always been and still am a very big Dan Kennedy fan as he is most likely one of the best marketers in the world. The problem is getting to Dan as in, you can't. And if by some chance you do, he is VERY expensive, and that is IF he agrees to work with you.

I knew Dan was most likely out of reach so I set out to find someone that knew the Kennedy "style" and most importantly, could provide PROVEN results. So, I jumped on Google and started to look for marketers. Now pay close attention. Do you have any idea how many thousands if not tens of thousands of results will show up in that category? Guess who popped up on the first page...John Mulry. Tell you anything?

Yes, THE John Mulry. Top selling author and marketing wizard. Now I had never heard of John as I normally stuck to my own backyard of Scottsdale Arizona and John being located in Ireland.

That being said, it literally took me all of 15 minutes to realize that John was the guy I needed on my team. Like I said, I'm pretty savvy at marketing myself and I know who talks the talk and who walks the walk. After a few e-mails and one phone call I knew John was my guy.

His cutting edge marketing strategies designed to bring a stampede of customers to your door REALLY WORK! He also doesn't use just one strategy like I did; he has dozens of tricks up his sleeve anyone of which can mean life changing money for you and your business. He IS a pro's pro and everyone in the industry knows it.

The other thing about John, which is very important to me, is his character. Be warned, the marketing industry is full of sharks and frauds that will steal your money in a heartbeat and think nothing of it. John is on the other end of the spectrum. John has lived up to EVERY thing he had promised and much more.

He is not cheap to hire. He is what I call, "reassuringly expensive" but as my dad used to say, "Buy cheap, buy twice". I look at it this way and recommend you do as well. Hiring John is an investment in yourself. You need an expert by your side to help drive customers and revenue to your business because without that, you have no business.

Successful entrepreneurs and business owners ALWAYS hire the BEST talent they can and you should be no different. John Mulry is YOUR guy!

Jim Toner - 27 Year Investment Real Estate Veteran, Author of the *Consumer's Guide to Investment Real Estate*, the forthcoming book *Send in the Wolves* and founder of www.creatingwealth101.com

Personal Journey of Discovery...

Before we dive deep into the DIRECT RESPONSE principles in this book I'm going to bring you on my personal journey of discovery. That discovery was one that introduced me to these principles in the first place.

I don't have time to tell you my whole story but I WILL tell you that a few years, I was a business analyst working long hours and without any hope for advancement. To get straight to the point, I packed it all in to start my own business.

(Via a lifetime of low self esteem, bullying, failure after failure, borderline alcoholism a year long trip of volunteering in South America, swimming with sharks, being rescued by helicopter, ending up in jail (wrongly) in Brazil and whole lot of massive action and change).

The full story of all of this is in first my book *Your Elephant's Under Threat.*

At the time (when I returned from my year of volunteering) my main passion was fitness so I started a fitness business. I quickly realised two things:

1. If I couldn't market my business I'd fail and
2. I was more interested in the marketing behind my business than the fitness.

I then discovered that I was not only more passionate about marketing; I was actually a hell of a lot better at it than most.

That's when the 'maverick' started to sprout.

I immersed myself in the world of direct response marketing, I started buying books, courses and attended events in London, Birmingham, Manchester, California and Texas.

That conference in Texas set the wheels in motion. Little did I know that conference would introduce me to someone called Dan Kennedy (and GKIC) in a much bigger way than I thought possible and become a twist of fate that changed my life forever...

The first time I ever really heard (I'd heard tid-bits here and there before) of Dan Kennedy and GKIC, I was over in a mastermind meeting in Liverpool and the two guys organising it Chris and Jon kept harping on and on about Dan says this, Dan says that, GKIC do this, GKIC do that.

In case you unaware, GKIC or Glazer-Kennedy Insider's Circle as it used to be called, is an international group founded by the famous marketing guru and *the professor of harsh reality* Dan Kennedy. GKIC's sole mission is to help small business owners prosper. To date, GKIC has helped thousands of local business owners achieve REAL RESULTS with their marketing and their businesses... even in down economies.

I'm GKIC's main man in Ireland and I'm the owner of the GKIC Ireland chapter. More on that later.

Back to how I discovered these strategies in the first place.

At that mastermind meeting, I could tell that they weren't really doing him justice so I took it upon myself to find out more about him. If you read or will read my first book *Your Elephant's Under Threat*, I'm a big (scrap that) a huge believer in three simple but powerful words:

Invest, Consume and Act.

I believe success comes down to investing in yourself, consuming what you invest in and then acting on what you consume. Sound's fairly simply and it is.

Well I'm also a believer in that if you want to learn something you might as well learn it from the best. So I decided to seek out Dan and GKIC. And to say it as concisely as possible, I'm delighted I did.

When I first encountered them and their strategies I was giddy with excitement. I started implementing and I started getting results and I was hooked.

I wanted more so I decided I'd go straight to the source. I wanted to get straight to Dan himself.

This isn't easy. He doesn't do email, use the internet and he only communicates via fax.

I know right?

So I needed to be creative and I needed to get his attention (first goal of marketing) so I needed to SHOW UP LIKE NOBODY ELSE (first rule of marketing).

I figured I'd do something different.

I knew Dan's surname was Kennedy which is obviously of Irish origin and being from Ireland I decided I'd put together a 'shock and awe' package for Dan.

A shock and awe package is a package that when you receive it you can't help but respond to it immediately. It's the ULTIMATE marketing tool. Nowadays I implement these for my clients but that's a discussion for later.

Inside the shock and awe package was a personalized authentic Gaelic scroll containing the meaning and heritage behind the surname Kennedy (it turns out he's a descendant from the first king of Ireland), a work in progress manuscript of my first book and very personal letter.

Did it work?

Well yes of course it did or otherwise I wouldn't be telling you this story.

Not only did it work and not only did Dan respond but it led to me becoming Dan's and GKIC's main man here in Ireland and one of very few Dan Kennedy trained Certified Business Advisors in the world.

So investing, consuming and acting on the strategies I was learning led to me being where I am today. My goal for you is to invest, consume and act upon what you read in this book.

I can contribute a lot of things to me investing, consuming and acting on GKIC's and Dan's strategies (one of which is meeting the love of my life Jess – best ROI ever btw).

How did Dan help me meet the love of my life?

It's pretty simple actually. One of Dan's core teachings is that you should BE SOMEBODY, BE SOMEWHERE and HAVE SOMETHING TO SAY.

Jess was starting out as the editor of SIN newspaper and she was looking for contributors, I seen the opportunity of writing for SIN, as a way to be somewhere and have something to say so I contacted her. We met, and the rest as they say is history... I'm a big romantic at heart :)

Today, I am fortunate to say I'm the author of the already highly acclaimed book *Your Elephant's Under Threat*, the top selling book *The Truth!* as well as this book *Direct Response.* I'm the owner of the Expect Success Academy, director of GKIC Ireland (the Irish arm of GKIC) and founder of *Thanks.ie*

Also, I have the good fortune of working with clients and members I choose to work with. And, I owe much of this success to Dan and GKIC and what their marketing and business techniques have taught me.

At this point you might be thinking so what and I get that, I really do...

I'll admit when I was in your position and when I first came across Dan, GKIC and these direct response principles, I was thinking exactly what you might be thinking this sounds way to good to be true, I won't have time to implement these strategies but most of all I thought, these strategies are from America, they won't work outside the US.

If you're thinking that, or whenever you start thinking about things negatively, ask yourself *"Where's the profit in that?"*

All I can say is well if you think that you know you're 100% right. Like Henry Ford says:

> *"If you think you can or you think you cannot you're probably right"*

Honestly, this problem of false thinking (which I'll discuss in detail later in this book) is one I've come up against again and again. You may not be in this position and you may be open to new ways of thinking, doing and acting BUT some people question my desire, alliance and unquestioning adoption of GKIC style marketing DIRECT RESPONSE marketing which I'll be outlining for you in this book.

They for whatever reason dismiss these strategies and claim they "won't work for their business". I know and my members and clients who are adopting GKIC style direct response marketing in their business know this isn't true.

The business owners I meet annually at GKIC events like the Infosummit and the Superconference come from all over the world including places like the UK, India, Nigeria, Russia even Israel (on average 1/3 of all attendees were from outside the US and Canada) also know nothing could be further from the truth. The thing is though; I was taking it all personal.

I took people's ignorance to new ways of thinking, their focusing on all the reasons why something won't work as personal but thankfully I don't do that anymore. I no longer try and convince the 'stubborn virgins' as Dan calls them to come over to the world of GKIC and adopt our DIRECT RESPONSE style strategies.

Not every business owner wants to fulfill their ambition...

Not every business owner gets it, I know that now. My job going forward is finding, nurturing and helping the ones that do. So to get the most out of this book you'll need the following traits:

1. You have honest ambition.
2. You're frustrated and disillusioned with not getting a ROI with your advertising and marketing.
3. You have a strong study ethic (you read books, study the best and constantly strive to improve)
4. You have strong work ethic (you don't expect everything to be handed on a plate)
5. You have the capability to implement what I will show you.

If you fit these five criteria then congratulations – you're a special breed of business owner and you'll love what I have for you in this book.

John Mulry

Asking Questions The Right Way

I love to meet other business owners and entrepreneurs.

It's great to hear their stories, find out what they do, who they serve, and how things are going.

I'm pretty good at getting to know folks pretty quickly and the reason is I'm more than happy to ask questions.

I'm a big believer in asking questions. You can learn a lot that way. About others. And about yourself and your own business.

But it really matters how you ask, especially when you're taking a good, hard look at your own operations.

Not only should you concern yourself with whether you're asking the right questions… you should get a bit more specific:

"Are you asking questions the right way?"

Here's what I mean.

All too often, I hear business owners asking themselves this kind of question:

"Why can't I get more customers?"

Consider how you're programming yourself for defeat in just the way that question is phrased. It presumes failure from the get go.

How would you likely answer this question? Well, if you're feeling defeatist, you'd probably say things like:

"The economy sucks."

"Nothing I try ever works."

"Nobody likes my business."

"Maybe it's a sign I should give up."

Talk about depressing!

By continuing to ask in that way, you're just setting your mind up for a litany of frustration, anger, and pain.

Instead, why not take the same question, but frame it like so:

"What specific steps could I be taking right now to generate more leads, more sales, and more ongoing revenue?"

Now that's a much better way to approach the situation. You're recognizing you want change and you're putting your conscious and subconscious mind into gear to come up with ways to make that change happen.

"I could try some new markets."

"How could I tweak my offer to make it better?"

"Let's try a new headline on my sales letter."

"Call up businesses that serve the same customers."

You see the difference? And it's all in how you frame the question.

But, of course, achieving greater prosperity in these difficult times is not just about asking the right questions.

It's about what you do with the answers.

It's about the action you take.

In this book, I share a lot of the questions you should be asking about your business.

I've included seven key principles and strategies that have been proven to work for many of my clients and they include many of the insights of my mentor Dan Kennedy – one of the world's most sought-after experts in marketing for business owners and entrepreneurs.

By the way, speaking of Dan, I want to share one of the most valuable tips I've picked up from him.

He said he developed one habit that he does every day. He's done it for over 30 years, and he still does it religiously.

Every day he does something to bring in business.

- Mail a letter.
- Call a business contact.
- Place an ad.
- Set up a lunch.
- Send a thank you.

Something. Every day. Big. Small. Doesn't matter. Every day he does something to bring in business. If you take just some of the actions I've suggested in this book, I'm confident that you'll start to see your prosperity increase.

For the best results possible, why not work out your answers and share them with me personally or share them with me at my local business group if you're local or in my Strategic Business Growth Club if you're from elsewhere.

You'll find more information about those when you get to the end of the book.

This book which in actual fact is more of a roadmap than a book is literally a step by step roadmap you can use to start marketing yourself and your business successfully.

Some of the material I present to you here may be new and seem a little out there. It's important when being presented with new information that you don't dismiss it because you have not encountered it before.

Within some chapters there are questions and exercises that you should take time to digest and answer. This will help solidify what you are reading and enable you to take in and retain more information.

The beauty of this book is that, once you have read through it in its entirety, you will be able to revisit each of the principles and APPLY them to your business.

I wanted to make this book as actionable as I've already mentioned I'm a big believer in investing, consuming, and most importantly, acting on what you consume.

The worst thing you can do is read this book through once and then let it sit idly on your bookshelf. Like I said, think of it as more of an action plan or workbook than a typical book.

A word of caution: typically the percentage of people that implement what they read is low. On average if you take 100 people who read a book, 80 of those will do nothing with the information, 15 will implement some and achieve some success, and 5 will implement everything and go on to great success. I challenge you to break this law of averages and go forth with the intention of implementation.

Finally, if you feel that you need help implementing or acting upon what you read, do not hesitate to reach out to me and apply for my coaching, marketing training or my done-for-you marketing campaigns. Visit www.JohnMulry.com to get started.

John Mulry, Msc

Principle #1: Define a Clear Message

John Mulry, Msc

34

"Success is predictable."
- **Brian Tracy**

One of the biggest obstacles to prosperity for most business owners is that they don't have a clear message to communicate to the market.

Somebody sets up a restaurant, a florist shop or coaching practice and they spend all their time and energy worrying about what it looks like inside or what their website is like.

Then they open the door and wait for the customers to come in.

However none of this matters if the customers don't show up.

You need to think about what you're going to communicate to the marketplace about who you are, what you do, what you're all about and why people should do business with you.

A marketing message is a way of concisely and clearly saying to the right market, "Here's what I'm all about, and here's how what I do can benefit you."

Most businesses fail to do this.

But when you take time to define your message clearly, your results will be so much better.

Here's an example. Two brothers started a little business as a means of putting themselves through college.

The concept was brother number one would run the business during the day and then go to school at night. Brother number two would do the inverse so that the business could get both of them through school.

A short while into this whole process, the business was losing money so they weren't meeting their objectives.

Brother number two essentially bailed out on brother number one. He took a used Volkswagen bug in exchange for his half of the business and drove off into the sunset.

Brother number one decided to stick it out and try and make something out of this thing.

Shortly thereafter, he developed a little company called Domino's Pizza. Domino's Pizza was driven by a marketing message which almost everyone knows.

That marketing message is, "Fresh hot pizza delivered in 30 minutes or less, guaranteed."

Keys to the Right Message

If you analyze that marketing message, you'll see some very interesting things.

First of all, it doesn't claim to be all things to all people. There is no mention of 'mama's recipe from the old country for special sauce'. In fact, there was not even any mention of 'good pizza'.

It's a wonderful example of truth in advertising.

All it says is they are going to get it to you while it's still hot and it's still fresh and they guarantee to do that.

That marketing message built an empire and a fortune for Tom Monaghan in a very short period of time and built a marketplace identity.

If you stop 10 people on the street today and throw the word 'pizza' at them in a word association game, seven or eight of them are going to immediately respond to you with 'Domino's'.

What you have to ask yourself is this. If you went into your marketplace, and stopped 10 people in the street, and you say 'flowers' or 'coaching' or 'restaurant' – or whatever business you are in – and seven or eight of them say your name, you're going to be doing very well indeed.

That's the power of a clear, compelling marketing message.

A Unique Selling Proposition (USP) is the part of the marketing message that differentiates you from your competition. It answers this question coming to you from your prospective customer:

Why should I choose you versus any and every other provider of the same product or service that you provide?

You simply have to have a good answer to that.

It's going to take a little bit of thought but, somewhere in your business, there is a good answer to that question (even if you need to make one or two changes somewhere).

ACTION QUESTION 1

Why should someone do business with you versus any and every other option available to them, including doing nothing at all?

_____

_____

_____

_____

_____

_____

_____

_____

By the way, if your answer includes things, like "I'm honest, ethical, keep promises, do what I say I'll do" etc... then start over.

If your USP contains things you should be doing and you should "be about" anyway, that's not unique!

The Importance of Widget Making

Another key aspect that separates the most prosperous businesses from the rest is that they develop the skill of widget making.

Widget making could be the number one skill you'll ever learn as a business owner.

Once you've got it, you use it over and over again every day in your business.

Widget making is where you take some of the products or services that you offer and present them to your prospective market in a way that makes it easy for them to buy.

On a real simple level, if we go back to the pizza business as an example, their widget of the week may be "two pizzas with double cheese for a special price".

They are not just saying, "Come and buy a pizza from us." They're holding up a specific thing and saying, "Here's our thing to buy."

On a different level, one of the best examples comes from Las Vegas in the hotel and casino business – where pretty much everybody offers the same thing.

Some years ago an entrepreneur took over one of the least successful hotels on the strip and had to find a different way to get people to come and stay in his hotel and gamble in his casino.

The widget that he developed was, "Give me $396 and I'll give you two nights, three days in my hotel in one of the deluxe suites. There will be a bottle of champagne waiting for you when you arrive. You can have unlimited drinks the entire time you are here and I'm going to give you $600 of my Dollars to gamble with in my casino."

So his offer includes the room. It includes the drinks. It includes several extras plus the $600 to gamble with.

That widget turned that struggling little hotel into one of the largest and most successful on the strip in Las Vegas.

The same approach is used in many other businesses.

There are really three reasons to use widgets and to base your marketing on them.

- One is to attract new customers by offering a free or low-cost widget to give them a chance to try out your services easily (like this book for example).

- A second reason is to sell more frequently to past and present customers by continually coming up with new and different widgets.

- The third reason is to move from the vague to the specific so that you can have something everybody can understand and grab onto that you promote.

ACTION QUESTION 2

What widgets can you create in your business? What can you offer that makes the decision to buy from you easy?

_____
_____
_____
_____
_____
_____
_____
_____
_____
_____

Communicating Effectively

Something that holds back many business owners is that they are concentrating so much on what they do, that they don't focus on how to sell what they do.

Let's say you're the best brain surgeon in the world.

Is this a valuable skill? Did you answer yes?

If you did, let me ask you if the skill is truly valuable or the application of the skill is valuable.

To get a better focus on this, let's ask this question.

If you're the best brain surgeon in the world, but you don't know how to get the word out about your skills, and you don't have any patients…is being the best really helping anyone?

Being the best, doesn't mean a thing if you can't apply your skills to help others solve a problem, fill a need or accomplish a goal!

There's a famous story about John Lennon where he said "Whenever we want one, I sit down and write a swimming pool."

That means he could sit down and write a hit song any time he wanted and could buy a new car, house, plane or swimming pool.

Exactly the same applies in your business.

If you can get good at something and then develop the skill of communicating effectively to others what you do, you can also write yourself a swimming pool.

In order to do that, you must be able to speak to people in terms of what it means for them.

Bringing Your Difference to Life

Here's a little exercise that brings that to life.

You take a stack of 3 x 5 cards and you begin to put one item, one feature, one fact about your business, product, or service; one idea, one theme or one item on each card.

Then you want to think in terms of all the features, all the benefits. Try to write a one sentence description of each one of those things as if you were going to write a headline for an advertisement about each one of those things; all the different ways that you could describe them. The more cards the merrier.

For example, to differentiate features from benefits, a feature of a dry cleaner would be same-day service. So on a 3 x 5 card, if you were building a case for a dry cleaner, you would write down "same day service."

Now you also want to be able to translate that into benefits.

One benefit that might go on the next 3 x 5 card would be that you can drop your clothes off on the way to work in the morning and pick them up on the way home from work that same afternoon.

One of the features that a lawyer might have would be a free consultation, a no-cost consultation with a client.

Now the benefit statement that he might choose to make about that is that you can come in and have your questions answered, and determine whether or not you have a viable case or a good solution to your legal problem, without committing any funds and spending any money.

Often, chiropractors will offer a free consultation or a free exam.

The benefit statement about that is that we can determine whether or not your health problem can be helped with chiropractic before you commit to a treatment program.

When you do that, you give each feature meaning and you personalize it to the individual's need.

Now you've got the basis of a great message AND you've got something the market will respond to.

If you would like to gain a deeper insight into how to put together marketing messages that sell – refer to my top selling book The Truth! (available at www.wrong.ie) or my free training at www.strategic.ie

John Mulry, Msc

Principle #2: Target the Right Market

"Failure is a success if we learn from it."
- **Malcolm Forbes**

One of the keys to crafting the right message is making sure you are aiming it at the right market.

The best possible offer made to someone who is wholly unqualified or wholly disinterested in it is not going to work.

You've got to match your offer with the right people to receive those offers.

You want to find good prospective customers for a business that:

- Can be reached affordably

- Are likely to buy

- Are able to buy

- Preferably already know you or are likely to trust you

You may think you know who your customers are but truth is we find this rarely bears out in reality.

Too many businesses have a tough time enunciating exactly who their customer is and what that person is all about.

This means they have a tough time producing advertising and marketing to reach these people.

A few years back, my mentor Dan told me he a story about a client he was working within the carpet cleaning business. This business owner was doing a lot of the right things in terms of crafting messages and using good advertising media. But he said none of it was working and couldn't figure out what was wrong.

They only worked out the solution when Dan took a drive with him around the area they were targeting. It was quickly obvious why he wasn't getting a good response from his reasonably good messages.

If you looked around the homes in the zip codes he was marketing to, the lawns were poorly kept, the yards were untidy, and many of the drives had old cars jacked up on them.

It was obvious these were not the kind of people who would be likely to pay money to have a carpet cleaning service come and clean their carpets.

He could have delivered the best marketing message. He could deliver a tremendous, irresistible offer – a great widget – to the people in that neighborhood and still get very poor response.

Right message, wrong market.

If you are in one of those areas, you short-circuit the whole process.

You're guaranteed to waste money and you are likely to have an abject failure of the marketing effort.

48

To get the right answer, you have to pick your target market with more sophistication.

There are several ways that most small businesses can approach this whole issue of target marketing.

For example you can target according to the geographic area, the demographics of the type of people, or the membership of an affinity group.

The more you know about your target market, the easier it is to identify them so that you can reach them with your message.

Start With "Who"

In fact, here are six words that will change your business life FOREVER!

Start with "who" then work backwards.

Too much of the time, we start with the "what."

- What do we want to sell?
- What do we want to promote?
- What service am I going to provide?
- What am I going to charge?

What? What? What?

The real question is, "WHO am I going to serve?"

Do you think it's important to know the age, income, likes, hopes, dreams, location, goals, problems, etc... of the people who are going to buy from you?

Do you think that, if you're selling Rolex watches, you better have the "who" you're selling to figured out before you write your message to them?

Could there be multiple "who's" that require multiple messages?

If one of your target markets is men buying an anniversary gift for their wives, do you think you might touch on different points than if you're trying to appeal directly towards a woman buying something for herself?

I'll just assume you agree.

➡ ACTION QUESTION 3

So right now, imagine one product or service you provide and describe "who" your ideal client, customer or patient is for what you offer.

_____

_____

_____

_____

_____

_____

_____

Then, for your next marketing piece, take this description out and write a letter directly to this person you've described...and ONLY to them.

So many people are afraid of leaving people out that they create generic, bland, boring marketing messages to everyone and no one at the same time.

You need to write to a specific person because...

There are "Riches in Niches!"

You move up the hierarchy of money when you move from generalist to specialist.

A simple example of this is; who gets paid more, the general practitioner or the heart surgeon? The "Astoria Yacht Specialist" or the guy at the boat shop?

ACTION QUESTION 4

So here's a way to work out how you can benefit from this approach.

What are four niches in your industry?

1. _____

2. _____

3. _____

4. _____

Now circle the niche you're in (or will be in after reading this.)

By being in a niche you'll have an 'idea' that makes you the ONLY choice for your ideal customer.

Taking Care of Your Existing Customers

We can talk a lot about targeting your ideal customer.

But there is one target market that is so often overlooked and it's literally a gold mine. It is acres of diamonds right in your own back yard.

This target market is your past and present customers.

This target market is the only one that clearly fits all of the criteria that we established before.

They can be reached affordably. You have their names, addresses and telephone numbers. You don't have to rent them. You don't have to buy them. You already own this asset.

They are likely to buy because they have had previous satisfactory experiences with you.

They are able to buy. They were able to buy before. They're able to buy again. They already know of you and are likely to trust you.

They represent the perfect target market.

Yet most businesses fail to make the most of it.

There are four big ways in which businesses miss out on this opportunity.

3. Lack of customer data

How many times does an individual buy from you or use your service and you're not able to continue to communicate with them because you do not know how to contact them?

The real value in any business is in the customer base.

It is 10 times easier to get existing buyers to return than it is to get new ones.

Plus returning individuals will spend twice as much per visit as new customers.

What would happen to your business if you had to constantly rely on selling new customers instead of existing ones?

So why do so many businesses not collect the necessary information to allow them to continue to market to the most valuable asset – their customers?

It's not just about the data you hold on your computers. It's sometimes about asking the right questions.

One printer we worked with had a client who came to him and got all of his letterhead printed there and all his envelopes and his business cards and little flyers and those kinds of jobs. He had been coming to him for several years.

One day that client came in and proudly presented our printer friend with a free copy of his new, beautiful, full-color 48-page catalog for all his products.

He had just had this printed by another printer and had spent a fortune getting it done and just wanted this printer to see it.

So our printer said to him, "Gee, why didn't you come to me to get that done?" The customer said, "But I thought all you did was stationery." All he had ever gotten done there was stationery.

He identified that printer in his mind as the place he goes to get his stationery. The printer had never probed and found out that this guy's business was a mail order business selling health and safety products.

The guy went through huge numbers of catalogs and full-color catalog sheets and product postcards.

Our printer friend was getting maybe $5,000 a year in printing business from this client. The guy was spending a half a million Euros a year on printing.

He never got any of it simply because he never got to know what that customer's business was all about.

Don't let that happen to you!

ACTION QUESTION 5

Identify five customers where you could find out a little more about what they do and see if there are further opportunities to work together.

1. _____

2. _____

3. _____

4. _____

5. _____

2. Lack of a Referral program

What is the second easiest customer to sell to?

Well the answer is a referral. Unfortunately most businesses live with the myth that, if they treat their customers well and give them great service, these customers will refer their friends to them.

Wrong!

The lack of a referral program is a huge marketing mistake.

The last thing that anyone is thinking about when they leave your office or store is, "Whom can I send to these nice people so that they can buy from them?"

It's not because they don't want to. It's because we're all too busy to be thinking about it.

That's why you need to have a customer rewards referral system in place which will give your customers an incentive to refer – while they're still in your office or store.

➡ ACTION QUESTION 6

What could you do today to get more referrals?

_____

_____

_____

_____

_____

_____

3. Lack of a Lost Customer Reactivation program

If a referral customer is the second easiest customer to sell, then who do you think is the third easiest customer to sell?

The answer is lost customers.

Again most businesses totally ignore the customers that have not been using their services for several years, when in fact these people are infinitely easier to sell than new customers.

ACTION QUESTION 7

What could you do today to reactivate old customers?

_____

_____

_____

_____

_____

_____

4. Too infrequent contact with present customers

So referrals and lost customers are the second and third easiest customers to sell to but, if you haven't already guessed, your present customers are the easiest.

The best way to accomplish this is to simply increase the frequency of your contacts with them.

It is amazing to me how many businesses think they can mail or call the customer too frequently.

You can but you're probably not even close. According to one survey, the proper frequency to contact your customers is every 20 days.

Perhaps even worse, for every month that you do not contact your customers, you lose relationship with 10% of them.

So wait 10 months and you might as well be mailing to the phone book.

One of the fastest ways to get an upturn in your business is to increase the rate of contact with the current customer base.

There's magic in increased frequency.

➤ ACTION QUESTION 8

What could you do today to increase contact with present customers?

_____

_____

_____

_____

_____

_____

_____

John Mulry, Msc

Principle #3:
Use the Right Direct
Response Media

"It may seem that those who do the most, dream the most."
-    **Stephen Leacock**

Alongside having a clear message and the right market, the third element that will determine the success of your business is the media you choose.

However, before you choose the media, it's important to be doing the right kind of marketing.

You should be doing DIRECT RESPONSE marketing.

This means that you can accurately measure the effectiveness of every single ad campaign down to the penny.

Why is this powerful for you?

Ask yourself, what ad campaigns you're running right now or have run in the past?

If I sat down in front of you and asked what each ad campaign brought in for you in terms of inquiries, customers and Dollars/Euros, could you tell me?

I could tell you this for each and every campaign I run and that I run for my clients.

So again, why is this so powerful?

If you knew that, every time you did a mailing campaign that costs $1,000, you got 50 inquiries and 15 new customers –

which directly generated $1,500 in profit – how often would you run that campaign?

Probably until the profit generated was lower than the cost of the campaign or until you found a campaign that worked better.

Perhaps you'll say that this type of marketing doesn't work in your business. Your business is "different".

But let me ask you four questions.

- Do you want more customers, clients or patients?
- Do you want them buying from you more often?
- Do you want them spending more (or do you want to charge more) each time they buy from you?
- Do you want them to give you more referrals than ever before?

If you answered yes to ANY of these questions then Your Business Isn't Different!

This approach works in all of the following industries and more:

- Retail (Bricks and Mortar and Online)
- Restaurants (Upscale to Fast Food)
- Service Industries (Real Estate, Carpet Cleaning, Plumbing and Trades)
- Professional Practices (Law, Medical, Financial, etc...)
- Business to Business (Service, Industrial, Staffing)
- Sales Professions (Mortgage Brokers, B2B Sales, Insurance)

- Health and Fitness (Health Club, Personal Trainers, E-Commerce)

In fact, every business and any business!!!

I can't stress this enough and quite frankly you're probably wasting your time if you're saying to yourself "But My Business Is Different."

You need to get out of this mentality if you're going to succeed.

The problem for too many business owners is that they fall into one of the following traps.

Trap #1: Being an Advertising Victim

The fact is that it's really easy to be an advertising victim.

You see, some advertising sales rep or agency comes by and tells you that you need to advertise because "you need to advertise". And they want to sell you institutional advertising instead of direct response advertising.

The difference is obvious. In fact, it's right in the name.

Institutional advertising is advertising like Coca-Cola, Dell Computers or Kellogg's. This is advertising where you can't measure your results.

They tell you that, when someone is ready for your particular product, they will now think of you and call you.

If you fall victim to this, you'll go broke.

The only companies that can afford this type of advertising are the Coca-Colas, the Dell Computers or the Kellogg's of the world.

What you want to do – and only do – is emotional direct response advertising. That's advertising where every Euro you spend is measurable and accountable.

Trap #2: Thinking You are the Customer

I can't tell you how many times I've had business owners tell me that their customers are too sophisticated for this type of marketing or this type of advertising.

This way of thinking without testing can be dangerous.

Just because you might not respond to something, it doesn't mean your customers won't and you need to be open to test new ideas.

➤ ACTION QUESTION 9

List the advertising and marketing activities you are currently doing and categorize them as direct response or institutional.

_____

_____

_____

_____

_____

_____

_____

_____

Choosing the Right Media

For most small businesses, there are the only three tools they're ever going to need to get their marketing job done.

If you want to use the tool analogy, you can build a whole house with these three tools. If you want to think of them as magic pills, which in some respects they are, you only need to take three pills a day.

There are three types of media, and media means the methodology we use to deliver our messages.

First, you need to be paid advertising online using things like Facebook Advertising or Twitter Advertising. Their targeting options are incredible; you can reach anyone you want.

In fact with Twitter and Facebook you can advertise directly to your competitor's customers or your competitor's followers and or fans. Genius stuff.

The second tool would be direct mail, and specifically, a three-step letter sequence that we use to zoom in on a prospective customer.

We keep going after that potential customer until they are compelled to respond.

The third tool would be content advertising or native advertising.

I know that a great many people have tried one, two or all three of these media, and have gotten unsatisfactory results.

There are several reasons for that – which has nothing whatsoever to do with the media itself.

It starts by jumping to the media without taking the proper steps to be able to use the media properly. You sabotage yourself before you get started.

Once you know how to properly use these three media, they consistently deliver the biggest bang for the buck of anything that you can possibly do to attract customers to a business.

There are two media tools that I put in the second tier.

One of those is small ads in newspapers, either your daily metropolitan newspaper or your weekly small town paper.

By small ads I mean ads that are only designed to get the telephone to ring, to get your interested prospect to raise his hand and say, "Yes that sounds like something I'd be interested in. Tell me more."

And then comes email marketing and email advertising.

Three Step Direct Mail

One of the reasons people think that direct mail doesn't work is they've only done one-shot direct mail. Because that's what everybody is doing.

That's why we put the focus on three-step campaigns.

You gain a tremendous marketing advantage in attracting people's attention and building interest and building a relationship when you go to the same prospect with a repetitive related sequence.

That sequence is extremely important. The first letter in the sequence might be several pages long but it's all about having the right message to the right market.

What happens is that the second letter in every sequence acknowledges and refers to the first letter, and the third letter acknowledges and refers to the second and the first letter.

When you have properly used the targeting mechanisms we've talked about – so that you are perfectly matching a message with a known-to-be-interested recipient – your odds of getting a lengthy message read and paid attention to go way up. The odds are way in your favor.

As a result, you can sometimes get phenomenal results either in terms of response percentages or in terms of Dollars/Euros back for Dollars/Euros spent.

We have achieved, not just once, but repeatedly, with long form sales letters, response percentages of 20%, 30% or even 40% from a relatively small list. We've done it because that list fits the criteria of a perfect target market that I laid out for you earlier.

The closer your match is, the more effectively you can use this type of marketing. These results can in fact happen for just about any type of business, given enough thought to make it happen.

Following the Direct Response Principle Online

I've focused mainly on the more traditional media because, in the current rush to go online, many business owners are neglecting the traditional approaches – even though these still work extremely well.

Nevertheless, online channels are growing in importance and will continue to do so – especially as the reach and power of mobile expands.

It's crucial to remember that the internet, mobile and social media are simply additional ways of achieving your marketing objectives. They are not some sort of magical solution in their own right.

The key to success in these – as in the traditional media – is having a clear message targeted at the right market and focused on encouraging people to take a specific action - such as giving you their contact details.

Of course this area is changing so fast and would justify a whole book on its own!

The pace of change means it's always a HOT topic in GKIC club and my Strategic Marketing and Business Growth Club.

Still Not Sure About Direct Response Marketing?

- **Direct response marketing is all about being measureable.** Do you want your marketing to be measureable?
- **Direct response marketing is about getting customers to respond immediately to your marketing.** Do you want customers to respond to your marketing immediately?
- **Direct response marketing is about knowing exactly how profitable each one of your marketing campaigns is.** Do you want to know exactly how much a given marketing campaign will make you?

Here are five doors opened when you use direct response marketing:

1. Use the same media everyone else is using…differently

2. Able to use media no one else uses

3. More opportunities to attract and acquire

4. More money spent wisely by eliminating waste

5. More time and energy to sell by eliminating frustration

Now are these five things you'd like to accomplish? Of course they are…so let's move on.

John Mulry, Msc

Principle #4: Think Like an Entrepreneur

"The horizon is out there somewhere if you just keep looking for it, chasing it, and working for it"

- **Bob Dole**

There is one big reason that so many businesses fail to achieve their potential and it's nothing to do with what they offer or how they promote it.

Let me sum it up in a question.

Why do so many small businesses fail when big stores like Tesco, Dunnes, Argos comes to town?

A. Giant companies personal service and knowledgeable staff?

B. Giant companies' high quality displays and attractive merchandising?

C. Giant companies' effective marketing campaigns and personalized follow-up?

D. Failure orientation of small business owners?

The truth is that all giant companies really have to do to dominate many markets is to stick a sign on a vacant piece of land saying "Giant Company Coming Soon."

When this happens many "Smaller One Man band" shops simply give up because they think that Mary and Tom, who've been buying from them for years, will simply switch over to Tesco because they can save .67 cents on a loaf of bread.

If this is the case, you're probably doing something wrong with your business to begin with (or you used to be before you read this!)

Failure Orientation is when people are controlled by external circumstances.

Next time you're bemoaning adversity, lack of resources or feeling you need to conform, these are signs of failure orientation.

Just ask yourself the same question I asked you to ask yourself at the beginning of this book "where's the profit in that?"

Successful people, when faced with adversity, see opportunity through creativity and action.

Successful people, when they lack resources, become resourceful and look for new ways to use old items, skills and people.

When everyone is racing to be the same, successful people find ways to do the opposite and be unique.

There's a reason I talked about a "Unique Selling Proposition" in the first rule and not a "Why I'm the same as everyone else" proposition.

Go from Business Owner to Entrepreneur

One of the reasons some businesses are so much more successful than others is that they are run by people who act as entrepreneurs rather than as business owners.

What's the difference?

Here's an example – and this is SO critical to your overall success.

- **Business Owner**: A jeweler who owns a jewelry store.
- **Entrepreneur**: A person who owns a jewelry store to build a list of customers and also has web offers, runs jewelry parties, organizes tours to diamond mines for rich clientele to pick their own diamond, has other luxury product stores and affiliate relationships with them.

So how do you move from one to the other?

Well, two different opportunities to go from business owner to entrepreneur are vertical and horizontal expansion.

Vertical Expansion

Vertical expansion is where someone buys (or re-creates) their vendors or the businesses they sell to. You go up and down the supply chain and buy those businesses.

ACTION QUESTION 10

So, what are five businesses you that you currently buy from or sell to that you could acquire? These don't need to be your current vendors or customers, they could be people you want to do business with or you could start that business.

1.

_____

2.

_____

3.

_____

4.

_____

5.

_____

Horizontal Expansion

Horizontal expansion is realizing that the real asset is the value of the relationship with the customer. You can buy or start related businesses that your list is already buying from.

This could be a restaurant owner who starts a catering business, an event planning service, a D.J. service, a professional photo shop, a wine store, limo service etc...

➡️ **ACTION QUESTION 11**

What are five businesses that your customers currently buy from that are somehow related to your business?

It could be price points, event driven, industry specific, current competitors who are slightly different.

1.

_____

2.

_____

3.

_____

4.

_____

5.

_____

Start with what the customer wants, NOT what you want.

The Miracle of 'Price Elasticity'

Read this carefully because it will change your business and life...FOREVER!

One of the biggest, most exciting opportunities in your business is the ability to sell at prices or fees substantially higher than you ever have before, than ALL your competitors, than your industry norms... even though you think you can't... and have more receptive, responsive, happier, more loyal customers, clients or patients.

Here are five reasons to embrace this miracle:

1.   More income per customer (annual customer value and lifetime customer value)

2.   More equity in your business

3.   More income per transaction, per product or per service

4.   More income from less work

5.   More respectful and appreciative clients

Let me ask you something that illustrates the effectiveness of this approach. Let's say you have 100 clients and each of your clients is worth $1,000 a year to you.

By embracing the concepts I'm talking about, you could increase the annual value of each client by 50% to $1,500 (and trust me this is not only possible, but on the low, low end of what's possible). You've now increased your income from $100,000 to $150,000 a year.

BUT… what if you lose clients by doing this?

Even when handled correctly, you will lose some clients when you raise your prices. So let's take a big number and say a full 25% of your clients leave you.

So now you only have 75 clients each giving you $1,500 each per year. You're still bringing in $112,500 (a 12.5% INCREASE from your previous income) a year and doing 25% LESS work.

ACTION QUESTION 12

Can you name three competitors (direct or indirect) who are selling a similar product for more money than you are? How much more?

1.

_____

2.

_____

3.

_____

Next to their names, write down how they are doing this.

Here's one quick tactic for increasing prices immediately. Take whatever you sell and create a "deluxe" version that costs 30% to 40% more.

Obviously choose things that either don't increase your costs or that increase them by less than the increase in price.

ACTION QUESTION 13

What could you add to your product or service to create a deluxe version?

_____
_____
_____
_____
_____
_____

By following this one strategy alone, you'll find that – if presented properly – a minimum of 20% of your customers will almost always take the deluxe version.

What would your business look like if 20% of your customers immediately started paying you 30% to 40% more?

Working On Your Business

One of the biggest problems we hear from business owners all the time is, "I'm too busy."

"I'm too busy to do any marketing because I'm the best salesperson and I need to be available all the time to my customers". Or, "I need to shop the market". Or, worse yet, "I need to parent staff".

The problem is you're working <u>in</u> your business instead of <u>on</u> your business. If there's one thing that you should write down and post as a constant reminder it's this…

Stop seeing yourself as a seller (or deliverer) of your particular product or service but as a marketer of your business that sells your category of product or service.

The marketer of any business will be one who achieves total financial freedom.

The real money is in the marketing not actually doing all the tasks within the business.

Setting aside time to work <u>on</u> your business instead of <u>in</u> your business will become the most profitable time that you spend during your entrepreneurial career.

Principle #5: Create Effective Systems

John Mulry, Msc

"You must do the things you think you cannot do."
- **Eleanor Roosevelt**

If your aim is to make your business as successful as possible, it's useful to look at what lies behind some of the world's greatest businesses.

The fact is that systems and processes are the life-blood of any great company or business.

Let's look at a couple of examples and see if you agree.

McDonalds…is one everybody knows. They have systems and processes for practically everything that could, and has, occurred in their restaurants.

Their systems are so well documented and their processes are so tightly organized you can plug nearly anyone into many of the positions in their restaurants and they will succeed.

Another one everyone's heard about is the assembly line. By having organized, sequential, operating systems, everything from cars to computers are made faster and better than ever before.

In all likelihood in your business you have some kind of operations system and procedure manual and can accurately provide high quality products or services time after time.

BUT...

I'd bet – if you are like most business owners – if asked to present your MARKETING system, you wouldn't have anything much to show me.

Marketing Systems

Do you have a marketing system?

If not, then what you have is money you spend (notice, I'm NOT using the term invest) on random acts of hope and faith (both often misplaced!)

Is that the way you should be running your business?

➤ **ACTION QUESTION 14**

To put a finer point on this, I'll ask you right now:

Based on your current marketing promotions, what are your sales going to be this week?

_____

Could you fill in a number that's at all accurate? If your answer is anything BUT a number, than your current system is one of hope and faith.

With a marketing system, you get to go to bed every night knowing what's going to happen in your business tomorrow, next week and next month with reasonable certainty!

But if you look around at all the business owners and sales professionals you know – probably yourself included – you will see people trying to achieve success by repeating accidents.

By random acts of marketing, getting erratic results – demand one day, no demand the next.

Being able to somehow find or attract several ideal clients this week, but having your time wasted the next with people totally unqualified to buy.

To escape this, you must have:

Reliable, Predictable, Consistent SYSTEMS That Affordably and Efficiently Provide Abundant Quantities of Quality Prospects, Customers, Clients.

By definition, a system is organized, reliable and consistent and therefore capable of delivering consistently predictable results.

This means you are NOT advertising or doing prospecting work wondering what the results may be; you know in advance as if psychic. That means you go to bed EVERY night KNOWING, within a small range of variance, what tomorrow will bring.

Let's look at the key components of that definition:

Affordability: Your marketing systems must deliver profitable results. You have to know what a customer is worth to you, then decide what you are reasonably willing to invest to acquire one, then build systems that work within that limit.

However, there's no free lunch, so if a customer is worth $1,000 and you're only willing to spend $10, you're a fool, and you might as well exit now; that's not how you build businesses and get independent and rich.

Efficiency: Your systems must be "targeted", to reach only those people most likely to buy; *High Probability Prospects*. Without this shift in thinking, you'll never achieve consistent affordability.

The more of the work that leads up to selling and developing a customer/client which you can put on autopilot – and have done for you by media (letters, websites, etc.) – the more of your time gets invested only in the highest value functions. So you make more money from less time.

Quantity/Quality: Whatever your income goal, it dictates a certain quantity of lead, prospect and customer flow, which requires a certain amount of investment.

You should know those numbers as they presently work in your business.

Now, by improving the "quality" of both the prospects selected and reached and the communication with them, you can change those numbers for the better... getting more from less.

Key Elements of Your Marketing System

Here are the key elements of a marketing system:

1. A selected group of prospects (sometimes referred to as a "farm", "farm area" or "target market"

The better the selection, the better the results.

For example, when you are able to analyze the response to a mailing list, you can identify those elements with the greatest chance of success and focus on those so that you get the best return on your money.

2. Appropriate media for best reaching those prospects

For some it might be direct-mail, and for some a big postcard; for others a personal letter in an envelope; etc., or it might be e-mail; it might be advertising in some newspaper, journal or magazine; it might be online advertising.

There is no good or bad media per se.

The question is always: *how can we best cut through clutter and gain the attention of these particular prospects?*

And, almost always, you want to avoid "one shot" marketing in favor of a sequence, often using more than one media.

3. A compelling message of strong interest to your chosen prospects

Get away from big, broad, sloppy, one-size-fits-all marketing messages.... and stop talking so much about your products and services; talk about THEIR interests, desires, fears and frustrations.

4. An "irresistible offer"

In getting new prospects to step forward, indicate interest, give you permission and an invitation to sell to them, this is often done by creating and offering 'information' of relevance to what you sell and of interest to the prospect.

5. A means of response and "capture"

Interested, 'high probability prospects' need easy, non-threatening ways to respond – you may use your regular phone number or a free recorded message line, a website, a fax-back form, a reply card, coupons; different options for different situations.

If driving people to a website to obtain the information you offer, be sure it "captures" as much of the person's contact information as possible.

6. Multi-step, short-term follow-up

The information should carry with it a second "irresistible offer" – tied to whatever next step you want the prospect to take, such as calling to schedule an appointment or coming into the office, showroom or store.

Then a series of follow-up "touches" by mail, e-mail, fax, and phone are tied to the expiring deadline of that offer.

7. "Maintenance follow-up" of unconverted leads

People who do not respond immediately – within your first few weeks of intense follow-up – may have many reasons for "maturing" into buyers more slowly.

There IS value in this bank of slow-to-mature prospects. They should continue hearing from you once to several times a month.

This is a "Rome that isn't built in a day" for most businesses, and you may be too quickly tempted to think it sounds too complicated or like too much work or not well suited to your business.

But this is the path to liberty, so it shouldn't be brain-dead easy or child's play simple.

By 'path to liberty' I mean this – and only this – it can transform a business (and, yes, ANY kind of business) from those random acts and erratic results of endlessly repetitive manual labor, cold prospecting or wasteful advertising to a business running on system.

Dealing with the "Sticktoitiveness" Problem

While this word isn't scientific, it is very real and it is the reason why most people fail at most everything they do!

Admittedly this one is a little harder to quantify, but many of the traits that make people successful are hard to quantify.

The bottom line though is this...if you never make a system and never give it time to work; you are going to fail at most everything in terms of business.

You need to create a plan, and then stick to it.

In order to develop more "sticktoitiveness" it's important to understand why most people fail to "stick to it."

Here are six reasons why most people don't "stick to it" and what to do about "it".

- **No reason for confidence in "it"**: If you're creating a new system from scratch without a guide and you've got little or no experience about why this would work, then it's easy to lose faith in "it." To combat this, use a system you know that already works for others!

  The most successful business people often "swipe and deploy" ideas that are already working and get coaching, mentoring or hire someone to help implement this system in their business.

  You can also read books, buy courses, attend live events or hire consultants to learn and create these systems.

- **No confidence in "self"**: Your past does NOT equal your future!!! So many people simply abandon plans because they've "failed" in the past.

  Once you truly grasp that your past failures are simply things you learned from and move forward, you will astound yourself with what you can accomplish.

- **Insufficient reasons to "stick to it"**: What is the best possible outcome of what you're trying to accomplish?

  Don't just write "make more money" or "save time" but write down what that money will do for you, or what you can now do with your extra time. Then write down why you want that.

Get to the reason behind the reason. Keep asking "what will this do for me?" and then you'll know whether there's a reason to accomplish what you're trying to accomplish.

- **Too hard to do "it"**: This is actually the best reason to do "it." People waste a lot of time and money trying to simplify something that requires a complex solution.

  If to accomplish your goal it'll require 20, 30, 40 steps...how many other people do you think are going to take the time to create this system?

  You'll have given yourself a business asset that is almost impossible to replicate. So roll up your sleeves and start building!

- **INIs (Ignorant, Negative, Influences):** The more people you tell about your plan, the more people you'll meet that will tell you why it won't work.

  Be careful about who you tell, because often people with the least experience in what you're trying to accomplish will offer the most advice or criticism.

  Get rid of these people as advisors and instead seek out people who've accomplished similar goals – and have been where you have been – who will provide educated, positive insights.

- **Isolation**: The entrepreneur is the loneliest person on earth. It's been said, "It's hard to have courage in the dark by yourself!"

So what's the answer to this? Easy, don't go it alone. Get people to come on your journey with you.

You can take someone inexperienced but working towards the same goal or, better yet, find or hire someone who knows the way and let them guide you!

ACTION QUESTION 15

Creating Your System

While we can't create your entire marketing system right now, I'd like you to list three areas around which a marketing system could be created. These could be ongoing campaigns around different products or services, different annual or season promotions or even a one-time event.

1.

_____

2.

_____

3.

_____

Principle #6: Get Maximum Value Out of Your Day

John Mulry, Msc

"Time is our most valuable asset, yet we tend to waste it, kill it, and spend it rather than invest it."
- **Jim Rohn**

One of the key secrets that separate the most successful entrepreneurs from the rest is how they take charge of their day.

It's vital to understand that time management is a common convenient misnomer.

Nobody can actually manage time – like money it has a mind of its own.

However, we can manage our allocation of it and, more so, the ways in which it is consumed or stolen by activities and by other people.

We can manage access, rules of engagement and choices.

There is no such thing as secret software or secret sauce that you're going to find behind any exceptionally productive person.

They all pretty much do the same three things:

1. Place themselves in environments conducive to productivity
2. Severely restrict distraction and interference

3. Hold themselves accountable for getting chosen things done within predetermined time slots

Most people do none of these three things.

Some at different times manage one or two out of these.

The problem is they often try to overcomplicate things.

Scripting your day

You could storyboard your day easily by having 3x5 cards tacked on a corkboard, having a legal pad divided into 15 minute increment boxes on the left side with space for notes on the right side, or using a piece of paper typed up on the computer.

The most important elements of a day script are:

- Having exact start and end times for every activity, task, appointment, meeting or phone call
- Defining the exact objectives for each activity involving another person

The script for the day is a minute-by-minute prediction of the way the day will play out.

Most people's work life varies – so some days there is not much of a script and the whole day might be devoted to one thing. Other days there may be 30 deadlines.

These days most people are overcomplicating their businesses, their marketing and their lives.

They are letting themselves be spread too thin over way too many things to try to do – thus diluting focus, energy and resources.

To be clear, we do favor complex marketing processes along with comprehensive and thorough monetization of leads and prospects. But that mostly involves systems which are engineered once and then operated.

The truth is most businesses or careers have five or fewer truly critical and essential success factors to focus on and organize everything around.

The list of things which you decide to ignore in order to devote enough energy to a shortlist is as important as the shortlist itself.

One secret of ensuring productivity is to make all your work Euro-constrained.

A given activity can only be allocated the amount of time its monetary or compensation value permits – if activities are permitted to eat more time than they pay for, you wind up missing income targets.

This helps rule out many things altogether; things many people have come to believe they must do without ever holding those things financially accountable.

One of the best things about tight scripting of the day is that nothing can consume more time than allocated to it because something else is starting one minute after the previous thing ends.

It is hard to waste time when there is no time to be wasted.

Consider the simple matter of phone calls – if a person engages in an average of four a day over 250 workdays, that's 1,000 in a year.

If, on average, they consume just 3 minutes more each day than you would have through tightly controlled end times and scripted days, that's roughly one whole week wasted – thus shortening your year to 51 weeks. In 10 years, that's 500 hours.

The same math would apply to time given to social media or repeatedly negotiating with an employee over his repetitive bad behavior.

In summary, here are some of the key lessons from the way exceptionally productive people work:

- Accepting that no-one can manage time itself
- Learning from the three things that productive people do
- Recognizing the importance of identifying and focusing on five or fewer critical success factors
- Refusing to be spread so thin you have no impact
- Knowing that what you choose not to do is at least as important as what you do
- Applying financial accountability

ACTION QUESTION 16

What are the five or fewer critical success factors that you should focus on?

1.

_____

2.

_____

3.

_____

4.

_____

5.

_____

Mistakes Entrepreneurs Make with Their Time

The reverse of what productive people do is the mistakes that so many entrepreneurs make with their time.

Here are five of the biggest mistakes:

1. Permitting others to dictate your agenda, schedule or way you work

Every successful entrepreneur I know has developed and adheres to a way of working that is productive for them.

Some are 'neat freaks' and have a full-time assistant doing nothing but filing. Others operate in controlled clutter with project files.

Some dictate, some use laptops, some still use legal pads.

Some go to the office on a regular schedule, others at random, others not at all.

The key issue is not being handed a set of "time management techniques" and forcing yourself to do them but to find time management techniques that work for you.

When you land on one, you refuse to be dislodged from it.

Everyone else must adjust or be gone.

2. Tolerating "time vampires" and others who waste their time

Successful entrepreneurs have very low tolerance for those who habitually waste time and disrupt productivity.

I suggest "three strikes and you're out".

Employee, vendor, even client: Explain why their behavior is incompatible with the way you work and/or interfering with your productivity and describe the substitute behavior desired.

Sit the vampire down for that talk three times.

Say: "Strike One, Strike Two, Strike Three – and you're out. Next!"

If you have vampires sucking your time now, make the list. Plan the talk to have with them on a 3 x 5 card with their name on it.

Go play baseball.

3. Permitting commoditization of themselves or services so they are weak and vulnerable and fearful in relationships with clients or customers

This is a fundamental power issue. If you are or feel commoditized, hustle and fix it.

Reinvent; alter your marketing; work like a fiend to put (perception of) supply versus demand, specialist versus generalist to work <u>for</u> you rather than against you.

Successful entrepreneurs do NOT operate from fear.

That's not really because they are fearless; but because they've created a set of circumstances for themselves that makes it easy to be fearless.

4. Operating without targets

Successful entrepreneurs use a lot of benchmarks, numbers, statistics, goals to hold themselves and others accountable, daily, weekly monthly, yearly, per project, per function.

5. Working in unproductive environments

Successful entrepreneurs are able to produce good results under adverse conditions – but strive not to be in that position very often.

Whether at home, in the place of business, travelling, wherever, whatever, they exert control over their environment, and give themselves every advantage to support productivity.

Delegation

In order to be able to manage your time to get things done that are important to you, you must first preserve some time to manage by getting your team members to get the things done that should be important to them.

This requires you to pass on responsibility to others in such a way that they understand, accept and are motivated to complete the work. This is the toughest part of management for most people. Very few people do it well.

There are a number of factors that influence the relationship between the manager and given employee that will affect the outcome of the delegated work - including personality styles, the overall work environment etc. - which can be covered in a short discussion.

However there are two certainties about delegating work:

1. The effort will fail if the individual lacks a full understanding of what is to be done

2. The effort will fail if a procedure is not in place and understood for checking work

Here then are seven questions to ask yourself to ensure the individual understands the assignment and that its completion will be checked:

- What is to be done?
- Why does it need to be done?
- Who is to do it?
- When is it to be done by?
- When is the doer to report on progress?
- How is the doer to report?
- What will constitute and verify successful completion - what are the desired results?

➡️ **ACTION QUESTION 17**

What five key tasks can you delegate to someone else today and what procedures are you going to put in place for checking?

1.

_____

2.

_____

3.

_____

4.

_____

5.

_____

To find out more about how you can get maximum value out of your day visit www.expectsuccess.ie/esp **to get my 'profit planner'.**

John Mulry, Msc

Principle #7: Build a Powerful Support Network

John Mulry, Msc

"You can get everything you want if you help enough others get what they want."
-   **Zig Ziglar**

The three key factors I'm going to cover in this final rule could quickly and singlehandedly double, triple or quadruple your income...

AND you're almost there already!

Modeling Success

This first one is modeling. Let me give you an example.

If you could become the best golfer in the world simply by watching videos of Jack Nicklaus, Tiger Woods, Phil Mickelson and Arnold Palmer, how much money and time would you invest to get your hands on those videos – knowing that after watching them you'd be able to replicate everything you saw?

My guess is you – or someone you know – would spend a lot of money on these because now you'd have the ability to make millions of Euros a year, playing a game in some of the most gorgeous spots on earth.

The problem is, it's not this simple when it comes to sports or physical ability.

HOWEVER...

When it comes to being able to duplicate success in business, it is that easy.

You can simply find models and then follow them. You'll need to invest time and/or money to get these models, but they are there for the taking.

You also have the unique ability to take parts from several successful systems in order to build your own successful composite model.

Finding a Mentor

Now let's talk about mentoring...

Behind every great person you'll more times than not find great mentors.

ACTION QUESTION 18

Name the three biggest influences in your life from the past and what they taught you.

1.

_____

2.

_____

3.

_____

ACTION QUESTION 19

Now name your current business mentors... these will be people who believe in you more than you do!

1.

_____

2.

_____

3.

_____

If you couldn't name any, you NEED to get one or more, qualified mentors right now.

There are a lot of resources for you online, but one of the easiest places to find qualified mentors is through GKIC.

Just contact us and we'll guide you to the right place based upon your needs, goals and experience.

Creating Your Success Environment

Sticking with the golf example, have you ever turned on the TV to golf and seen a player who's about to tee off? Close your eyes for a second and picture that scene in your mind.

You probably envisioned someone in funny looking clothes concentrating entirely on what they were about to do.

You also saw others around that person, spectators and officials alike, working together to provide that golfer with the best success environment possible by staying as still and as silent as possible.

What does your office, your business, your mind look like compared to this?

The final principle I'm going to share, that will help you increase your income is the need to have an environment that frequently and consistently gives strategic reinforcement.

You need the power of a place where the ambitious striver...the creative visionary...the starter-of-many-things...the serious student... the wealth seeker is NOT "odd" or ridiculed and criticized!

You need a place where these people congregate, learn and grow, collaborate, are encouraged and celebrated!

At a minimum, you need to be listening to CDs, reading newsletters, meeting with like-minded individuals, attending live events and constantly giving yourself a consistent message about what you're trying to do.

My final thought will be this...but it's an important one, *"What is dominating your thoughts controls what you get!"*

▶ ACTION QUESTION 20

So now write down here what you want to get, what you really, really want AND why.

_____

_____

_____

_____

_____

_____

_____

_____

_____

_____

When you have done that, put it on your wall so you can be super-focused on what's truly important to you.

So now you've gone through this book and you're ready to take action on what you've just discovered.

Your creative juices are flowing… business building ideas are coming fast and furious. You can't wait to do whatever it takes to change your business, your life and possibly even the world.

That's exactly as it should be.

However, I don't mean to rain on your parade, but… have you ever felt this way before? Yet you still find yourself here… so I have to ask: "What's going to be different this time?"

What are you going to do so that six months, one year, five years from now you don't find yourself in the same place once again?

Running a business on your own... without any proven support network in place for advice, ideas, and ongoing feedback and motivation... can make true transformation incredibly hard to achieve.

Fortunately, we have a solution to that all-too-common problem... you'll find details of it on page 167.

The 'Direct Response' Collection...

On the following pages you'll find a collection of 'how to' style chapters that will help you implement the strategies of this book. Some of these chapters may contain some overlap to what we discussed. This is on purpose. I want to hammer home the principles so they will sink in.

These chapters are as follows:

- How To Make Sure Your Advertising And Marketing Gets Results. Period.
- How to Get More Customers With Lead Generating Advertising That Works!
- How to Increase Profits WITHOUT Getting More Customers
- 8 Ways To Generate Business From Networking Events
- 99 Questions EVERY Business Owner & Entrepreneur NEEDS to answer

How to make sure your advertising and marketing gets results. Period.

"It's much easier to double your business by doubling your conversion rate than by doubling your traffic." – Jeff Eisenberg

Your marketing materials are an extension of you and your company. How are yours working? You can have a lot of fun creating marketing materials for your business. It's an opportunity to work on a project that isn't a spreadsheet, or a graph or an order form.

You can really get creative!

Your materials get distributed in the world to send out a particular message (or messages) about your company and what you sell. They're ambassadors for your business because they speak to your potential customers when you're not there.

As you probably know, it's easy to get carried away with marketing collateral. You're surrounded by flashy, clever advertising everywhere you look, and when the time comes to create your own, you can't help but feel that you have to keep up with the joneses.

Most of the time this doesn't work.

You spend more money, and see less impressive results. In this post, I'm going to show you some proven strategies for simplifying and strengthening your marketing materials, and focusing on the materials you need not the materials you think you think you should have.

In this comprehensive chapter (which is an excerpt from my top selling book The Truth! By the way) we will cover:

- The marketing materials you really need – and the ones you don't
- The mistakes you might be making now
- The elements each piece of marketing collateral should have
- What you need to know about the design of your materials
- What you need to know about testing, measuring and making mistakes

It's easy to want to match your competition piece by piece – but when you're trying to stretch your marketing budget, focus on the materials you actually need.

Just because your competition has an eight page, glossy color brochure, doesn't mean you need one to run a successful business.

And the same goes for any online marketing materials or properties too.

When one brochure has the ability to eat your entire budget for marketing materials, you have to prioritize what's essential and what's just a "wish" or want.

You need to make sure you're spending on the items that are going to bring in the most return on investment.

Your marketing materials need to communicate your message to your target and motivate them to act. Do you really need a glossy brochure when black and white flyers will be just as effective? Think about this when making decisions about your marketing items. Make choices based on how your target audience prefers to receive information.

- Do they prefer paper newsletters, or electronic ones?
- Are they environmentally conscious, or technology savvy?
- Do they appreciate personal contact, or just need to see information in a newspaper?

Remember that how you communicate is often just as or more important that what you communicate.

What are the marketing materials that your business needs, wants and would like to have?

- Logo
- Business Cards
- Brochure
- Website
- Marketing funnels
- Social Media Accounts
- Newsletter
- Catalogue
- Advertisements
- Flyers
- Fridge Magnet
- Branded Swag (pens, etc.)
- Employee Clothing
- Cloth Bags
- Product Labels
- Signage
- Email Signature
- Blog
- Letterhead + Envelopes
- Thank You Cards
- Notepads
- Seasonal Gifts
- Company Profile
- Internal Templates (Fax Cover, Memo, etc.)

Create a list of your essential marketing materials then, below it, create a list of your "wish" marketing materials. You can use your "wish list" when you have a little extra budget, or are looking to create a "wow" piece. The list above is for you to use as a guideline – you may not need all of these items, or want to add your own ideas to the list.

Take your existing marketing materials through this audit, and look for opportunities to improve and strengthen.

Are you fighting for their attention with a powerful headline?

Like I talk about in my book The Truth! you have about four seconds to grab the attention of your reader with your headline. If you do, you have a few more seconds to convince them to read your sub-headline. If you're successful in doing that, you have a few more seconds to get them to read further. See what I'm saying?

Make sure your headlines:

- Offer to take away pain or give pleasure
- Hit your target market's hot buttons
- Bring up emotion
- Are bold, dramatic, shocking or unbelievable
- Answer the questions – what's in it for the customer? Why should the customer care?

Are you triggering an emotional response to a problem, fear, need or want?

Once you have their attention, you need to continue to keep it. Shake up their confidence in what they're doing now, or the urgency with which they need to solve their problem. Put their fears, concerns and desires in black and white text in front of their eyes:

Ask them if they:

- Are doing enough?
- Can wait any longer?
- Can sacrifice anymore?
- Are paying too much?
- Are getting the best product or service for their money?
- Are you building their trust or confidence in your ability to meet their needs?

You've got their attention, and tapped into their emotions, now you need to build their confidence in you ability to solve their problems and meet their needs. You'll need to show them your solution, and prove that you can be trusted to do what you promise.

Tell them how:

- You're different from the competition
- You're highly qualified
- You have documented results
- You have a high number of happy customers
- You get recognized from others in your field

Are you wowing them with your competitive edge?

You may be the best at what you do or have the best product but if your customers can't get a hold of you when they need you, how valuable are you? Here are some examples:

Tell them how you do more than the competition:

- 24-hour customer service
- Housecalls, or free delivery
- Customer rewards program
- Other convenience services

Are you overcoming their objections before they've raised them?

It makes no difference what business you are in; there will always be objections to buying what you are selling. Most often the biggest objection is the price. You should confront them head-on by explaining why it's worth paying your price. You need to put their fears to rest before they will be ready to buy.

Are you providing an element of risk reversal with a strong guarantee?

Stand behind what you're claiming about the quality of your product or service, and offer a guarantee in your marketing materials. Typically, the strength and length of the guarantee indicate the quality of the product in most customers' eyes, so create a strong one.

You can guarantee:

- Performance
- Benefits
- Longevity
- Satisfaction

Are you showing them what other people have said about your product or service?

Use testimonials to speak to your credibility and merit. Let the testimonials show your potential clients how trustworthy you are, and how much benefit they've received from your product or service. Make sure the testimonial addresses the problem that your customer had before they used your product.

Are you giving them an easy way to contact you?

Make it easy for customers to be in touch with you, or get more information. Clearly display your phone number and website address on everything you produce, and consider including a map of your store location so you're easy to find.

Are you giving them a reason to act NOW?

The last job your marketing piece has to do is motivate your viewer to take action. You need to make them want to call for more information, visit your website, or just come into your store. Invite them to take action on every page.

To motivate customers to act, you can:

- Offer special "bonus" offers to quick responders
- Make a time-sensitive offer
- Tell them how rare your product is, or what limited quantity you have
- Offer limited-time added value

Are you telling them what your product or service will give them?

Your customer doesn't care about the features of your product or service, they only care about the benefit that feature will provide them. Customers buy benefits, not products or services. A client is looking to buy some more confidence from a new hairstyle, not a haircut.

Are you telling viewers the story of your product or service?

Remember that you are painting a story to tap into the emotions of your viewers. Detailed technical descriptions should be replaced with descriptions of how the customer may enjoy the benefit, and how they might feel.

The story will help the reader picture:

- How they'll feel after using your product or service
- What they'll look like using your product or service
- What they'll have time to do once they buy your product or service
- The relief they'll experience after purchasing your product or service

Are you giving them a reason to keep your marketing piece?

Give your customers a reason to keep your business card, brochure, newsletter or direct mail piece, refer to it, and pass it on to others to see. For example using shock and awe packages like I mentioned at the beginning of this book.

If you are selling hair care products, you can give your readers tips on how to combat split ends, frizz, unruly curls and heat damage. If you sell kitchen products, you can provide recipes that use your cookware or tools.

Some ideas for keep-able marketing pieces are:

- Top 10 lists
- Tips for product caretaking and longevity
- Recipes
- How-to's

Flashy design is not important to your marketing campaign – but clear and professional looking materials are absolutely essential.

When it comes to the visual presentation of your marketing materials, you need to strike a balance. On one hand, you don't want to spend all of your budget on design and production. On the other hand, the cost of sending out materials that don't look and feel professional is usually much higher.

If you're going to try something new – test, measure and make mistakes in small batches, or online.

You will need to constantly be monitoring the success of each piece of marketing material and looking for opportunities to strengthen and improve it. Since you already have your lead tracking and management system in place, this is a matter of sitting down on a regular basis and reviewing the leads each piece generated, and how many turned into sales.

Remember, always test, measure and then make choices.

If you're not sure about a new strategy, do a test run to a limited distribution area, or test the message out online. Do small production runs of brochures or flyers you're not sure about, so you don't end up with heaps of flyers that didn't work.

In the end, the strength of your marketing piece is in what you say and how you say it.

I'll say that again.

The strength of your marketing piece is in what you say and how you say it.

Too often, flashy design gets in the way of the message and you miss an opportunity to attract a customer. Simple, clear marketing materials deliver an easy-to-understand message to your target audience, and result in far better results and a far better experience for your target audience.

If you want to dive deeper into this then I highly recommend you get a copy of my top selling book *The Truth!* Or reach out to me personally.

How to get more customers with lead generating advertising that works!

Leads are the lifeblood of your business whether you get them online or offline the bottom line is you have to get them.

Every conversation I've ever had about a struggling business results in a conversation about lead generation...

The late Jim Rohn had a quote that said:

"there are stories of the beholds and the bewares... make sure you're part of the story that is a behold."

He also is known to have said:

"You have to get good at one of two things... planting in the spring or begging in the fall."

Planting in the spring is the same as getting, either online of offline, clients. If you're not good at planting... getting clients, you'll surely be begging,... relying on price not value, and taking short cuts to make a sale, etc.

That is why today, we're going to focus on lead generation; we're going to make sure you don't have to go "begging in the fall!" we're going to show you how to get a steady flow of prospective clients.

So let's examine the ingredients of a Lead Generation Ad done right, as demonstrated by this case study (see ad below)...

So what are the BASICS of effective Lead generation?

Well, Instead of advertising your business, products or services...

You advertise FOR the person you want to attract....

By offering a free information or 'widget' that is specifically created to be irresistible only to that person OR an implicit benefit (like in this case study ad above).

What are the BENEFITS of this style of lead generation?

A small ad in print, online media, a simple postcard or coupon can do the work of larger more expensive media...

It builds your prospect list for follow-up...

Question: What free information could you offer that would be irresistible to the person you want to attract?

_____
_____
_____
_____
_____
_____

Six Crucial Elements That makes This Ad Brilliant!

Okay, so there are six specific elements of this ad I want to examine with you.

- THE "CALL OUT" OR "IDENTITY" HEADLINE.
- "DOG WHISTLE" LANGUAGE
- CLARITY / UNABASHED SPECIFICITY.
- ONLY WHAT IS NECESSARY & NO MORE or (NOT GETTING AHEAD OF YOURSELF).
- The TAKE AWAY.
- RESPONSE DIRECTIONS.

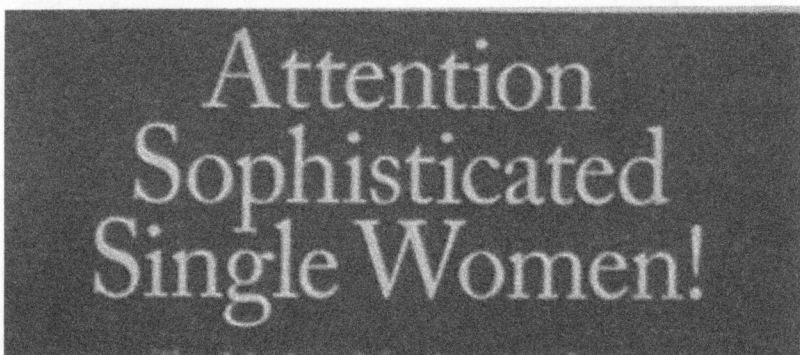

Attention Sophisticated Single Women!

Let's begin with the first one, the "Call out" or "Identity" Headline. This headline immediately tells readers who should respond and who should not.

Most advertisers are unwilling to do this because:

1: the fear of turning away anyone...

2: they fail to design a business that is "for" anyone in particular...

Question: What "call out" headline could you use for advertising?

_____

_____

_____

_____

_____

The second element is the "Dog Whistle Language"

It's written to convey meaning to certain people that others would not grasp (like a dog whistle that is heard only by dogs, not by humans.)

The dog whistle examples from this are:

- Women are described as "Sophisticated" and "Well Kept"
- And Men are described as "Professionals" and "Elite"

Just a word of warning, a Common Advertising Problem is not choosing an ideal prospect to attract. This means you cannot tailor your advertising or marketing. You're stuck with "anybody" language.

Question: What word choices could you use that would make your ideal prospect think "Hey! This is for me!"?

_____

_____

_____

_____

_____

The third element is the Clarity and Unabashed Specificity. In other words you need to be precisely clear in describing who you want to respond. Examples from this ad include the following words…

- Engaging
- Attractive
- Single
- Aged 40-60
- Active
- Well-built
- Well-kept
- Non-smokers
- Enjoys cultural activities

Also look at the picture choice: It's of an affluent, older man in a suit, grey hair!

Another Common Advertising Problem is not deciding on your ideal prospect. When you don't do this your ads will be too general…

Question: What are three words to describe your ideal prospect you could use in an ad?

_____

_____

_____

_____

_____

The fourth element of this type of lead generation is it gives only what is necessary & no more...

There is nothing about the company except name, logo, slogan (AND they COULD HAVE even SKIPPED THOSE!)

The advertisement does not say...

How long in business
Number of successful relationships
Background of founders

The lessons here are:
- Don't get ahead of yourself!
- Don't try to make one ad do too much– lead generation AND brand building is too much

Question: What can YOU take out of your current ads and still have it work for lead generation?

_____

_____

_____

_____

_____

The fifth element is the fine art of Take Away Selling...

There is a gentle but present, overt "If you qualify" message.

You must be willing to offend some to attract your ideal prospect. It is OKAY to INTIMIDATE, REPEL AND OFFEND if it attracts with precision...

In this ad, Words that say who qualifies are:
- Sophisticated
- Engaging
- Attractive
- Single
- Aged 40-60
- Active
- Well-built
- Well-kept
- Non-smokers
- Enjoy cultural activities

Question What other kinds of advertising "take away" are there?

_____

_____

_____

_____

_____

Two answers are (1) a Limited time offer, and (2) – limited supply.

The sixth essential element your lead generating ad should have is...

(1) A benefit so good and obvious you don't need an offer as is with this ad...

OR (2) an irresistible offer

So what is a good offer? Well it must BE PRECISELY MATCHED TO the AUDIENCE!

Free information is usually a good choice. Things like...
- Reports
- Books
- Videos
- CDs
- DVDs
- Specific things to read, view or retrieve online.

Finally Response Directions Should be Simple and Direct...

Do NOT clutter up a lead generation ad with a bunch of different paths and things to do like: follow us on TWITTER, FACEBOOK, LINKED IN, YOUTUBE. It will convert a lead generation ad into a sloppy mess.

Question: What irresistible offer can you make to prospects?

_____

_____

_____

_____

_____

So there you go, the six essential elements of a lead generation ad when done right.

How to Increase Profits WITHOUT Getting More Customers

Would you like to know some effective ways to increase profits in your business WITHOUT getting new customers?

Without knowing who you are or what business you're in, I can tell you that with near certainty that there's a massive source of untapped revenue sitting in your business. Where is that untapped revenue? It's from your existing customers.

In this chapter I'm going to give you 15 ways to increase profits and extract maximum value from your own customers.

Russell Conwell, who was one of "the forefathers of motivational speaking", had one lecture he loved and gave the most. It was his 'Acres of Diamonds' lecture and he delivered it more than 6,000 times. This lecture wasn't some fantasy, it was a true story he heard in Iraq.

His speech made the point that most people look everywhere for opportunity, happiness, etc. except under their own feet, where they are most likely to find it.

This translates to one of the greatest secrets of making money and one of the best ways of increasing profits via marketing: virtually every business owner fails to fully mine the gold in his own customer list, every retailer fails to mine the gold in his own neighbourhood, every restaurant owner fails to mine the gold in his restaurant, etc. while constantly scrambling for the next lead, the next prospect, the next customer.

The core asset in your business...

The biggest challenges I hear from business owners is: "I need more leads", "I need more customers" or "I need more clients".

They have no qualms about going out to spend hundreds if not thousands of Dollars/Euros a month on Google Adwords, Social Media marketing, newspaper ads, radio ads, flyer drops, you name it but then they baulk at the cost of doing a monthly mailing (printed, not email) to their existing customers.

Another one of my mentors Jay Abraham literally built his fame and fortune by going into established businesses and helping them maximise their core asset: their own customers. The beautiful thing is you don't have to spend $25K to go to one of his seminars to get this strategy.

Here are 15 ways to increase profits, and extract maximum value from your own customers:

#1. Offer more products and services – "the mini-conglomerate theory"

No matter what business you're in, there is at least one (but likely many) more products or service you could be offering your customers.

For example, if you're a personal trainer and you encourage your clients to take supplements, rather than them buying their supplements elsewhere couldn't you sell them?

Or if you sell bouncy castles for kids birthdays parties could you also do clown hire or face painting? The best thing is that your customers are more than likely buying these products and services anyways so they might as well buy it from you right?

#2. Make offers to them more often.

Another misconception is that you should get a customer to make a sale. The proper thinking is that you should make a sale to get a customer. Once you get that customer as long as what you're offering them is coming from a place of value you could and should keep offering them more and more consistently and repeatedly.

Now, the pre-requisite here is that you're not selling snake oil and you don't constantly bombard your customers with just offers.

#3. Reward frequent purchasers.

You probably have some customers that pretty much buy everything you have to offer right? What have you done lately to reward those customers. Have you called them up to tell them you appreciate them? Have you sent them a thank you card (yes, a physical card, not an email)?

If not, you should, people love recognition, and something as simple as a call or card will go a long way.

#4. Reward high-volume purchasers.

Similar to above, how are you currently rewarding your high volume purchasers? Have you a system for 'bumping-up' single purchasers to multi purchase? You can do so easily by offering incentives for higher purchases and then rewarding those customers that buy more often.

#5. Incentivize greater usage.

What can you offer your customers to encourage them to use your product or service more often? Have you a client that you're seeing maybe once a month but you know that they could benefit meeting you more often? Have you communicated this to them? Could you come up with a bonus offering to your customers for when they use your products more often?

#6. Create "VIP" groups – i.e., memberships with special privileges.

People, no matter from what background love exclusivity and love to feel a sense of belonging. Do you currently have a membership or group income stream in your business, and if not why not? Having a "VIP" group or membership is a fantastic way to add massive value and monthly continuity income to your business.

This can work for any type of business a coach, trainer, restaurant, hairdresser, retail store, coffee shop, and while it involves some work, the benefits are well worth it.

#7. Learn more about each customer, and tailor offers to match.

How much do you actually know about your customers? For them to become customers in they first place they obviously know, like and trust you but just how much do you know about them? The more you can find out about your customers the better.

When you know exactly how they think, what they like, what they dislike you can make tailored offers to them. But equally if not more important you can start to clone them and find prospective customers similar to them.

#8. Communicate frequently... with information, education, even fun (not just another pitch).

Related to point number two, you need to make sure that you communicate frequently with your customers. You could (and should) send them useful information, articles, newsletters (online and printed), educate them on your business offerings and even send them some fun stuff.

One thing you want to avoid is constantly sending them pitch after pitch. While this may bring results in the beginning, you'll quickly burn through your customers and word will spread.

#9. Communicate consistently – you build relationships with regular communication, not haphazard.

You also need to ensure communicate consistently. How frequent this is will be different for each business, if you decide to communicate every day then stick to every day. At the bare minimum I would say keep in touch with your customers at least once a week and preferably using multiple media.

For example I communicate with my customers via email twice per week, once a month via a physical mail and once a month in person at my monthly seminars.

#10. Analyse your customers and separate them into A-B-C groups based on responsiveness, then develop strategies to upgrade Cs to Bs, and Bs to A's.

Look at your customer list, have you a pocket of customers that buy higher priced products and services and another pocket that buy lower priced products and services. These are two different types of customers (when it comes to describing them in terms of your ladder of ascension).

You should separate your customers based on their responsiveness (for example "A", "B", and "C") and communicate with them separately and develop strategies to move your Cs to Bs, and Bs to As.

#11. Identify and focus like a laser on hyper-responsives
Some percentage of your customers will buy.

EVERYTHING you offer. Make sure to give them plenty of chances to do so. We all have mavens in our business. When you identify them and focus on them you can add more value to them and offer them more products and services while at the same time finding out more about them so you can replicate them thus adding even more value and profits to your business.

#12. Sell continuity programs that provide regular, predictable cash flow.

A lot of online marketers and agencies say "content is king". I disagree, wholeheartedly, continuity is king. If you don't have continuity income in your business currently, you are leaving massive amounts of profits on the table.

For example:

- If you're a book store owner you could have a book of the month club.
- If you're an online coach you could have a monthly membership site.
- You could do monthly paid seminars regardless of your business.
- If you're an organic farmer you could have a weekly box scheme.

No matter what business you're in, continuity programs enable you have regular, predictable cash flow which will be a breadth of fresh air if you always seem to have more month at the end of the money.

#13. Sell renewable products or services.

As it's said: "if it doesn't go down the drain, it ain't a business". What can you offer your customers that needs to be renewed? Using the personal trainer as an example, if he's encouraging his clients to take protein powder and take omega 3 fish oils these are:

- products he could be selling,
- renewable products meaning that once they are used up the customer will need to buy again.

Imagine the impact on your business if you're customers happily bought from you again and again.

#14. Become "the Go-To Resource" in your category for your customers — use and leverage strategic alliances and joint ventures.

How many times have you been a "connector" for your customers? As you find out more and more about your customers (point number 7) you'll discover that may have needs or desires outside of your business.

By collating the information, leveraging strategic alliances and joint ventures you can become "the Go-To Resource" in your category and elevate yourself in the eyes of your customers and pretty much eradicate your competitors.

#15. Periodically ask/survey your customers to find out what else they want and would buy from you.

How often do you ask your customers what they want? Do you periodically survey your customers to find out their pain points, their frustrations, their needs, their desires? Doing so systematically can and will enable you to find out exactly how you need to be innovating your business on an ongoing basis.

Peter Drucker the "founder of modern management" said the two most important things in business is marketing and innovation and your current customers can hold the key to you constantly innovating and improving.

Most business owners and marketers drastically underestimate their customer's capacity to consume more of their products and services. The bottom line is you should be absolutely doing more business with your existing customers versus chasing new ones.

Remember: a buyer is a buyer is a buyer is buyer. It's infinitely easier and always more profitable to work at increasing the purchasing of your satisfied customers than it is to go out and add new ones.

What are your light bulb moments from this list of 15 ways to increase profits and extract more value from your existing customers? Which one gave you your biggest 'aha' moment?

How are you going to apply this to your business?

_____

_____

_____

_____

_____

_____

8 Ways To Generate Business From Networking Events

Do you go to Networking events?

Would you like to be consistently able to generate business from networking events?

If so read on…

Networking is a word that you either love, something you see as a necessary evil or something you hate completely. Personally I'm only a fan of networking when it's done right and in the right environment.

I'm a 'right message, for the right market' kind of guy and networking can be really effective way to not only connect with other businesses and people but also an effective way to actually get sales (the reason we're in business anyways).

However, in saying that, networking can be, well let's be honest, boring and a complete waste of time.

To ensure you get the best out of your networking activities here are eight strategies you can use to be more effective at networking…

1. Know your end game when networking.

You wouldn't believe the amount of people I've spoken with who go to networking events with absolutely no idea why they're going or what they'll do when they get there. What's the goal of going? Is it to build connections? Is it to meet that hard to meet guy you've been trying to reach for months? Is it to meet a potential partner? Is it to get free wine and cheese?

No matter what your goal is, don't go networking without a goal in the first place.

2. Don't be that guy when networking.

Years ago I was at a networking event having a conversation with two gentlemen who for the life of me I can't remember who they were (they left a lasting impression obviously) when another man came roaring up like a bull in china shop and literally flung his business card in my face, blabbered his name and then proceeded to go to everyone else in the place doing the exact same thing.

DON'T be THAT guy.

Going around handing out business cards to anyone and everyone is not networking; it's just being a pest. Especially if what's on your business card is of absolute no value to me (but that's a topic for another day). You don't get business by being a pest; you get business by being a welcomed guest.

3. Do your research BEFORE networking.

Like point number one where you should know your end game, you should also prepare. I know you've heard the saying' fail to prepare and you better prepare to fail'. It doesn't matter how many times you heard, it you don't heed it, you need to hear it again.

The great thing about networking events and summits like the Infosummit and the Superconference is that you find out ahead of time who is going so you can prepare ahead of time.

If there's a big account that you've been chasing for months and you know they're going to be in attendance you can do some research ahead of time to have an entry point.

This doesn't have to be difficult. Google, Linkedin and Facebook make it so easy to find out pertinent information on your target market and while the majority of people don't bother doing research before any networking events the ones who do are the ones who stand out and get noticed.

This is a good thing.

Imagine the decision maker of that big account you're chasing is attending an event and leading up to the event you research him (or her) and his (or her) company. In doing your research you find out that he just had a baby, his second, he posted happy pictures of the new arrival on his Twitter, Instagram and Facebook, little Molly, the bundle of joy.

Does this give you something to speak to him about? It sure does. You could say something like:

"Oh hey Tom, congrats on the new arrival. You'll have you hands full with Molly now."

This opens up the conversation and dialogue very nicely. But don't just jump from there into business, which leads me on nicely to strategy number four.

4. Don't be all about business when networking.

If you're goal of networking is to drum up business – great, but it doesn't mean you have to go in there hammering everyone over the head with how great you are (they don't care).

Networking is social meaning and can be most effective when you don't even mention your business (until asked). Make connections, ask the right questions, ask social questions. Ask things like:

- What do you do to unwind?
- What challenges are you facing?
- Have you any hobbies?
- Are you a member of any groups or clubs?
- These types of questions open up opportunities that cannot be opened by being overly formal.

5. What's your elevator pitch?

By elevator pitch I don't necessary mean your 30 second power sentence on your business in the traditional way. They're boring. I mean can you sum up in one sentence what you can do for me. Note I didn't say what your business is or what you do for a living, can you sum up in ONE sentence what you CAN DO FOR ME.

Take me for example. I don't say: *"I'm a marketing consultant."*

I say: *"I can help you get more customers, referrals and profits and maximise the ROI from your advertising and marketing spend."*

This automatically leads you to thinking: "how the hell does he do that?" When you speak to your target market do they think that? Start speaking in terms of what you CAN DO for someone instead of what you actually do.

6. Follow up after networking.

Connections are made with networking; sales are made in follow up. I just made that line up but feel free to quote it as long as you give me credit. Kidding aside, follow up with people after you meet them at a networking event.

Don't be lazy here. If you meet someone who could be potentially worth thousands of Dollars/Euros to you, would it hurt you to spend $2 sending them a thank you card (yes an actual thank you card)? They certainly won't be expecting it and they will not forget you.

Yes email is easier, yes an instant message is easier but that's what everyone else is doing.

7. Listen when you're networking.

Greek philosopher Epictetus said it perfect when he said: "We have two ears and one mouth so that we can listen twice as much as we speak." If you go to a networking event be it the All-Ireland Business Summit or Superconference or somewhere else make sure you listen more than you talk.

And actually do listen, don't just pretend to listen.

8. Don't waste your time when networking.

This last point may seem a little harsh but it needs to be said. Don't waste your time with people of no consequence to you. Time is finite and if you're stuck talking to someone who's not in your game plan chances are you're missing the opportunity to talk to someone meaningful.

Don't be rude and don't blatantly ignore them but be polite and say: "excuse me, it was very nice meeting you but there's someone I want to catch while I have the chance".

Like I mentioned, networking can be a fantastic tool for your business when it's done right. I hope these eight points' help you become a better networker.

99 Questions EVERY Business Owner & Entrepreneur NEEDS to answer.

Here's a list of 99 questions that will get your creative juices flowing faster and harder than Niagara falls and enable you to THINK better about your business.

No matter what stage you're at in your business EVERY business owners needs to take time to think about their business. This isn't wasted time or unproductive time – this is time well spent.

Why these questions?

Like I mentioned at the beginning of this book, I love asking questions. I love learning from people, learning how they tick, learning how they achieved what I want to achieve.

But most of all, I love asking potential customers, clients and business owners questions. It helps me learn more about your needs, your desires and what challenges I might be able to help you with.

Take for example of you go to my consulting website www.JohnMulry.com I've designed it around your needs and ask you a series of questions based on what you want.

Not on how great I am.

Answer the 99 questions below and I know for a FACT you'll get a burst of ideas, creativity, content and excitement about getting more customers, referrals, profits and more... Don't just read them. Answer them. Visit www.directresponse.ie/99q to download a handy workbook to help you answer them.

1. What keeps your potential customers up at night?
2. Can you describe your PERFECT customer?
3. Your WORST customer?
4. What questions do you get most often from customers?
5. What's a dirty little secret in your industry?
6. What's your favourite customer success story?
7. What's the funniest/craziest thing that ever happened to you in your business?
8. What's your personal business philosophy?
9. What's the best reason for a customer to NOT do business with you?
10. What can you teach your potential customers to do (for free) that would help them solve a chronic problem?
11. Are there other services, providers, products that you can recommend to your potential customers?
12. Is there "conventional wisdom" in your industry that is just plain wrong?
13. What things is your company NOT good at?
14. How and why did you get into the business you're in?
15. What's your most embarrassing failure story?
16. What lies are told in your industry?

17. What do you find yourself complaining about most?

18. What's your favourite part about coming to work everyday?

19. Look through customer emails for the last 6 months. Do you see any patterns? Any great stories? Any complaints you handled well?

20. Can you do a recording for your potential customers? Video? Mp3? CD?

21. Can you write a cheat sheet?

22. Can you email your list and ask them what they would like to read about?

23. If you have more than one list (more than one product/service) do have a message in each AR (autoresponder) series that offers your other product/service?

24. What is the most common exaggeration in your industry? How can you use understatement?

25. Do you have a blog...if so, what's your most popular blog post?

26. Have you been interviewed for a radio show? Newspaper article?

27. Has your company been mentioned on TV? Trade publication?

28. Have you written a white paper? Free report? Checklist? Guide? Instruction manual? Book?

29. If you were to survey your list, what would you ask them?

30. Who are/were your mentors?

31. What email subject line would ruin your business?

32. What is your greatest non-business success?

33. What was the last trip/vacation you took?

34. What is the next step you'd like the reader to take? How can you make it easier for him/her to take it?

35. If they've downloaded a free report, white paper, or ebook, have you spoon fed the most important principals back to them in email form?

36. Think of the most recent current event/pop culture reference that captured your attention. Can you relate it to your business? Can you make a contrast between the way the world" thinks and the way your potential customers think?

37. What's the most profound story from your personal life?

38. What is your most profound "Eureka!" moment when you finally "got it"?

39. What's the biggest mistake you ever made in your business?

40. Have you ever "fired" a customer?

41. What is your business "motto"? Do you have a phrase or famous quote you find yourself saying to yourself, your co-workers, your family?

42. Can you interview (either in person, on the phone or thru email) an expert in your industry or a related field?

43. What's the most earth-shattering claim you can make about your business?

44. What's the saddest experience you've had that you learned the most from?

45. What's the most common misconception your potential customers / customers have about what you do?

46. Have you ever walked away from short-term money because you knew it would cause long-term problems?

47. What's the earliest/most favourite childhood memory you have of being interested in your business or in business in general?

48. What's your favourite childhood memory...not business related?

49. What are three character traits that you have in common with most of your customers?

50. What problems do you face that your customers also face?

51. What's your favourite "war story"?

52. Who has been your most hated "enemy"?

53. What's your most gruesome war story?

54. What are your potential customers' idiosyncrasies?

55. Who are your potential customers' heroes?

56. Who are your heroes?

57. If you were to compare a customer's (or your) success story to a fairy tale or famous movie...which one would it be?

58. What is the boldest challenge you could make to your potential customers?

59. What's the sweetest deal you could make as a last ditch effort to get a reader to buy?

60. What was your last job before this one? What did you learn there?

61. What are the characteristics that separate the winners from the "wanna-bees" on your list?

62. What's your favourite "paid your dues" story?

63. In what ways does the 80/20 rule apply to your business/industry/reader list?
64. What's your favourite song? Novel? Movie? Painting? Poem? Sculpture? Play? Joke? TV Show? Why?
65. What businesses do you admire? Hate?
66. What advertisements do you admire? Hate?
67. What do you want your customers to say about you to their friends? Business associates?
68. What's the geeky-est thing you've ever done? A time where you just got lost and obsessed?
69. What's your take on the latest industry news?
70. What's the FUNNEST thing about doing business with you?
71. What "negative" about you is actually a positive thing about you? Ex: for financial planners "I'm boring, so that you don't have exciting times with the REVENUE Commissioners!"
72. What are the biggest costs your potential customers will incur if they don't do business with you (put dollar/Euro figures to them)?
73. What analogies do you find yourself using the most when discussing your business?
74. Do you have special procedures, policies or people that make you unique?
75. What are your business goals for this year? Next year? Five years?
76. What's the most outrageous guarantee you can make?
77. What's the dumbest thing a customer ever did?
78. What is your favourite "downtime" activity?

79. What are the three main reasons your product is so expensive? So inexpensive?
80. Can you create a "gold level" membership for your customers?
81. What do your competitors say about your product/service?
82. What's the best thing you can say about your toughest competitor?
83. How did you land your first customer?
84. What's the most "imperfect" thing about your product/service?
85. If you had to make a list of 99 things, what topic would you choose?
86. What does your spouse know better about your business than you do?
87. Would you recommend your children pursue a job in your industry?
88. If you were king of the world, what 3 things would you change about the world (or your industry)?
89. What is/was your worst character flaw?
90. If you were to segment your customers into 3 or 4 "types" what would they be?
91. If you could slap your potential customers upside the head and get just ONE idea through their thick skulls, what would it be?
92. If you had to give a speech at your industry's trade show, what topic would you choose?
93. What's the most common reason that customers DELAY doing business with you? Do you have "I wish I had done this sooner" testimonials?

94. Can you promote a product as an affiliate?
95. Why don't you carry a notepad and pencil with you at all times?
96. Can you run a contest?
97. Can you ask potential customers to beta test? Take a demo? Or a test drive for a reduced rate?
98. If you had to send an email message every day for 30 days, what would you write about?
99. What's the one BIG IDEA you've taken from these 99 questions?

About John Mulry

"Helping entrepreneurs grow their business and profits through successful   online and offline direct marketing systems."

Biography:

John Mulry is an award winning and trusted marketing advisor, speaker, and top selling author with a unique, deep knowledge that spans both online and offline direct response marketing.

He helps business owners get more customers, referrals and profits through his consulting, his done for you marketing funnels, his training courses, books, strategic marketing club and private business group in Galway.

When John first started his business rather than accept the status quo of the impending doom of the recession he sought out and has studied under some of the most world-renowned experts in business, direct response marketing and coaching.

Experts including marketing legends Jay Abraham and Dan Kennedy, GKIC, lifestyle and business experts Tony Robbins, Dax Moy, and Emmy award winning movie director/branding agent Nick Nanton.

He lives and breeds by his creeds "invest, consume and act" and having an "expect success attitude". John was handpicked by Dan Kennedy and is Ireland's only GKIC Certified Business Advisor.

John has been featured as a guest contributor on numerous publications including Business.com, TweakYourBiz, NUI various newspaper and publications as well as been a guest speaker for the SCCUL Enterprise Centre, OMiG, JCI Galway, Galway Chamber of Ireland, the Elite Performance Academy, All-Ireland Summit, Plato and the Ennis Business Network.

In February 2013, John launched first book Your Elephant's Under Threat which received worldwide acclaim from some of the top business and marketing experts worldwide including: top selling author Brian Tracy, world renowned sales trainer Tom Hopkins, Infusionsoft founder Clate Mask, celebrity branding expert Nick Nanton as well as his own mentor and founder of GKIC, Dan Kennedy.

In May 2014 John won the JCI TOYP (Top Outstanding Young Persons Award) and has been a finalist in the JCI Young Entrepreneur of the year, OMiG marketer of the year and blogging awards.

In April 2015, John launched his second book The Truth! – which hit the top sellers three days in a row and received acclaim from customers and clients the world over. He has also launched numerous training programs, courses both online and offline.

For more information on John and how he can help your business visit www.JohnMulry.com

Also From the Author

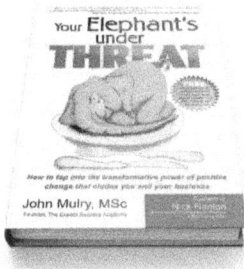

Your Elephant's Under Threat:
John's highly acclaimed first book details his journey from lost, alone, with no direction and living someone else's life to drawing upon the transformative power of positive change within him and the others he surrounded himself with. He changed his life, found happiness, has a business that serves him and now with the information, systems and strategies he shares in this self improvement book, you can too....

Praise for Your Elephant's Under Threat:

"If you're an entrepreneur who's struggling to adapt to the changing world of business or you need a system for defining and getting exactly what you want in life, then you need this book."

- **Brian Tracy International, Legendary Speaker, Trainer and Author of over 60 Best Selling Books**

"The thing about John that most people aren't willing to do, is to actually APPLY the best practices that they learn to their own business and life in order to achieve maximum effectiveness in minimum time. I love the fact that John lives and breathes what he teaches in this book. One of the most important concepts that surfaces in his book is summarized in his three words: INVEST, CONSUME and ACT. If ever there was a simple definition of how to succeed, John has 'nailed it' with these words. Moreover, he's living proof that the invest/consume/act model works."

- **Nick Nanton, CEO of the Dicks + Nanton Celebrity Branding® Agency, Emmy Award Winning Director, Producer & Best-Selling Author**

"In order to achieve success in life, you must first expect it, define it, and apply knowledge gained through education and experience. John Mulry's book, Your Elephant's Under Threat, is an excellent tool to use on your journey."
- **Tom Hopkins International, Speaker and Author of How to Master the Art of Selling**

"What a fantastic, straightforward, and honest book backed by a WONDERFUL story of positive change. If you are an ambitious entrepreneur and want to have your own story of personal triumph and business success, read this book!"

- **Clate Mask, CEO and Co-Founder of InfusionSoft**

"John Mulry's personal story and journey is provocative and profound...He has revealed a lot about personal and business transformation, making it an organised process rather than an accidental evolution."

- **Dan Kennedy, Author & Marketing/Business Strategist**

To get your copy visit www.JohnMulry.com/elephant

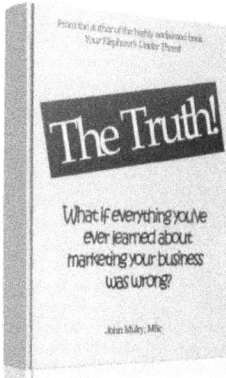

The Truth!

This is more than a book advertising and marketing from one of the leading trusted marketing advisors of our time. It is a book by a man who helps successful businesses become more successful.

It is a bible of tested techniques for anyone interested in creating profitable advertising and marketing – based on empirical evidence from over 200 industries.

And it's one of the most exciting business books you'll ever read.

From John:

"The Truth! isn't just a book, it's a step by step system for marketing your business. It's the book that I wish I had when I first started my business. What I've put together isn't tactics or tricks to work now and then, or it isn't based on one particular media like social media or whatever, it's based on the unchanging principles of human psychology and how people make buying decisions.

I've put it together to be more of a blueprint than just a series of chapters, each one build upon the previous and the end result is a system you'll be able to deploy in your business for attracting your ideal customers."

Praise for The Truth!

"It didn't take long for John's marketing gems to click on a few light bulbs for me and set me straight, as I put together my new advertising campaigns."
  - **Doreen Mellor**

"My mind was blown away by the in-depth business concepts, strategies, tactics, tools and honesty I saw. Before I met you I didn't have a easy to follow and implement system"
  - **Frederick Chelogram**

"At last someone has made an easy actionable blueprint for success, in any niche, without all the fluff and BS. John has made it fail proof not to succeed in business, but only if you get off your butt and put in the action."
  - **Kevin Long**

"Really helpful, broke everything down into simple to understand, bite sized chunks that helped me get over the fear of marketing."
  - **Pol Murray**

To get you copy of The Truth! Visit www.wrong.ie

The 'Place' For Prosperity...

John Mulry, Msc

Your Invitation to 'The Place For Prosperity'

Boom. You made it this far. Congrats. Many don't even open books let alone read them so congrats for coming this far. This REALLY is just the beginning. Now it's time to take things to the next level.

I want to send you this shiny gold packet (okay it mightn't look shiny in the above picture but trust me it is) of brand new and unreleased trainings that myself and GKIC are using as a shameless bribe and gift to get you to test drive the GKIC Gold Monthly Membership.

Now I'll tell you about that in a second but first let me show you what I'm using to bribe you.

The 1st program I'm giving you is the **Lifestyle Liberation Kit.**

Magnetic Marketing
Lifestyle Liberation
Kit and Welcome Kit

This kit comes with a manual, 3 CDs and a flash drive and inside you'll learn how to go from a business that owns you to a business that gives you the freedom and control to enjoy your life.

Do you ever feel trapped by your business? Do you ever feel like you're working with clients, customers or patients who aren't your most ideal clients?

Do you also ever wonder why it is your competitors who aren't any better at what they do than you are seem to have it easier and they seem to have more freedom in their business and in their lives?

Well in the Lifestyle Liberation Kit we walk you through why that is and how to overcome it.

The training that's inside this kit might just be the secret weapon to you taking your business from where it is today to where it is you want to go. Wherever that place this training will help you.

I know you're going to love it.

The next gift I'm giving you is access to NINE detailed training's over nine weeks showing you how to transform your business from ordinary to extraordinary.

The first training is all about **maximizing the value of every customer of client you have.**

Most businesses focus on selling their one core product…that's it. In this training you'll learn what you should be doing instead.

Training number two is all about **getting clarity about what it is that you want in your business**…and what you don't want.

This is where you'll paint a picture of what your ideal day looks like in your business and personal life so that you have a goal. That way you'll know where you're headed so you can accurately build the roads that get you there.

Training number three is all about **how to make an offer your prospects cannot refuse.**

That way you're not out chasing prospects...but you're attracting them like a moth to a flame.

Training number four builds on the previous and shows you how to flip the model so that your **potential customers are pursuing you, not the other way around.**

Training number five is all about **cloning your best customers** so you can focus on working only on those who are the most qualified and who you actually enjoy working with.

The sixth training is how to implement the **force of the marketing triangle** in your business.

In training number seven you'll discover **how to make yourself the most obvious choice in the eyes of your potential customers.**

In training number eight you'll discover **how to start automating processes in your business** and implement systems that free up your time and money.

And in training number nine you'll find out **how you can hold all of your advertising and marketing spend accountable** so you're no longer wasting money on advertising and marketing.

As you can see those NINE trainings alone are pretty irresistible but that's not all you're getting your shiny gold packet...

You'll also get an exclusive welcome kit that contains your first issue of the No BS marketing letter which I'll talk about in a second, a special three step plan for implementing what you'll learn, a special behind the scenes look of how and why some of our most successful members are thriving as well a handy wall chart to keep you on track.

But that's not all of it either, like I said it's a big bulky gold packet...

You're also going to get our tools and resources catalogue and the No B.S. Income Explosion guide. This is a guide and intro to the place for prosperity. It details what you should be focusing on and how to get the best results possible with everything you'll get both now and in the future.

At this stage if there was nothing else you'd be hard pressed to find an offer or shameless bribe as irresistible as this but we want to go above and beyond and ensure your success.

Inside your shiny gold packet you're also going to **receive a complimentary ticket with a real life value of $497** to one of our live implementation bootcamps which are a two day events where we sit down with you and actually help you implement these systems in your business.

These bootcamps are run by the chief marketing officer of GKIC Dave Dee as well as Mike "*The Jewel*" Stodola.

In fact let me spend a minute to talk about these bootcamps...

It was actually one of these bootcamps that has me where I am today. Remember at the start of this book I talked about going to an event in Texas. That even was a GKIC Fast Implementation Bootcamp.

Like I mentioned, going to that event was one of the best decisions of my life as it led me to where I am today, it put the wheels in motion to help me achieve my goals, made me realise what I truly wanted and it helped me go after it like a man possessed.

You're going to get a free complimentary ticket to attend one of these very same bootcamps. In fact these are so good; I plan on attending some more myself in the future.

As you can see this is one hell of a packet to receive right?

Like I said myself and GKIC want to send you this entire packet for FREE as a shameless bribe for you to try the GKIC Gold Monthly Membership.

GKIC Gold Monthly Membership

Here's what's included in your membership.

1. Access to a private thriving online community including powerful networking opportunities with

other entrepreneurs and free online access to all your member marketing tools.

2. Our monthly No B.S. Newsletter delivered to your door loaded with fresh tips from Dan Kennedy and GKIC experts on vital topics for all small business owners. You'll also receive a digital copy too of this powerful actionable newsletter.

4. A monthly marketing interview on CF highlighting actionable steps from some of the top minds in the business.

5. A monthly marketing hot sheet with actionable tips for every business owner.

6. And member only discounts on GKIC conferences and seminars that provide invaluable opportunities for members to drive their businesses forward and network with like-minded entrepreneurs.

Here's how much everything "costs"

We're going to send you everything in this fancy, shiny gold packet for absolutely FREE.

And that includes shipping to anywhere in the world.

You're getting everything, the kit, the trainings, the manual, CDs, flash drive, poster as well as the complimentary tickets to the Fast Implementation bootcamp which have a real world value of $497 all as a shameless bribe to try out your first month's membership of the GKIC Gold Monthly Membership. Plus we'll even send you a binder to keep everything together and organised so you can store future issues.

If during your "try us out" month you decide you don't want to stay a member, then let us know by phone or email or cancel from within your member's area.

If you choose to stay a member after your initial month, it's just

$1.99 per day

…Which adds up to $59.99 per month

Not expensive but enough to ensure that only ambitious, forward thinking business owners will take advantage of it.

Now here's the part where I'm supposed to tell you that this is the best thing since slice bread and it's going to make you a tonne of money.

I won't do that, what I'll do instead is…

Something profoundly different…

How about we let everything speak for itself?

You're getting the Lifestyle Liberation Kit free with your initial month.

176

If you don't think that the kit along with everything included in your first months membership isn't worth at least 10 TIMES the investment then email, call or cancel online.

Plus you can keep everything you've got. You don't have to return anything, you don't have to jump through hoops – just let us know and it's a done deal.
Everything you get is yours regardless.

That way the risk is 100% on us.

Visit www.directresponse.ie/gold to avail of this shameless bribe.

So there you have it.

You're getting the manual, CD's, flash drive, trainings, complimentary live event ticket as well your No B.S. marketing letter today as a shameless bribe to get you to test drive the GKIC Gold Monthly Membership. All of these "bribes" are yours to keep for free anyway – just for taking a look.

Thanks again for reading this book but also reading this special invitation and I look forward to welcoming you into this community, this place, for prosperity.

Sincerely,

John Mulry

GKIC Certified Business Advisor

Remember, if you remain a member it's just $59.99 which is just $1.99 per day.

You can't get a whole lot for $1.99 a day.

At the time of writing, an Americano in Starbucks costs $2.45.

You probably drink one or two cups of coffee/tea or some sort of drink each day right?

So let me ask you... which would you rather have?

¾ of a cup of coffee or the latest most cutting edge marketing strategies delivered right to your door... accompanied by a growing thriving community of like minded entrepreneurs?

Obviously the answer is a no brainer...

Accept our bribes today and just say "MAYBE"

If this is right for you... you'll know immediately...

If it is, forego the $1.99 and stay a member...

If it's not, simply cancel. And keep everything anyways.

Visit www.directresponse.ie/gold today to join us.

Direct Response

John Mulry, Msc

www.ingramcontent.com/pod-product-compliance
Lightning Source LLC
Chambersburg PA
CBHW022038190326
41520CB00008B/631